T0247654

# BEYOND NO

ERIK NAGEL

# BEYOND NO

HARNESSING THE **POWER OF RESISTANCE** FOR **POSITIVE ORGANIZATIONAL GROWTH**

WILEY

*For my wife, Dorin, who believes my choice of wardrobe is an act of resistance against good taste.*

*For my daughter, Yma, who gently ignores my attempts to resist her autonomous handling of curfew.*

*For my son, Maxim, who thinks I should chill out a bit more anyway.*

# Contents

# Introduction

"Yes, you're right. There is always resistance," said my counterpart, a renowned communications expert. Then after a brief pause for thought: "But I must admit … I prefer it without the resistance." At that, we both had to smile.

Resistance stands for a very difficult part of organization, management, and leadership. It does not have a good reputation. Often, pockets of resistance or particularly unruly individuals cause concerns or trouble for management by behaving in a non-sensical, irritating, or even destructive manner. With this under-standing, resistance is then ignored or eliminated.

I take a different perspective in this book. Everywhere in an organization, resistance arises in very different and often inventive ways, sometimes more, sometimes less subtle. Resistance is a stroke of luck. It makes something clear, brings something to light: objective differences, dissatisfaction, criticism of procedures, different assessments or values. Those who resist have – from their point of view – good reasons for behaving in this way. It is worth taking a serious look at the background to resistance: what exactly has happened? What is it about? What are the actual concerns? Who made what contribution to the resistance? This more-detailed reflection on resistance promises unexpected insights and broadens the scope for action.

1

All members of the organization experience resistance, exercise it, feel challenged by it, endure it, or deal with it. Resistance is therefore not only a concern for managers, but also for project managers and technical/administrative employees. In this respect, the book is aimed at all those people in organizations who want to take a closer look at resistance. Resistance is a particular issue in management and leadership relationships. However, this does not only apply to managers, as all those involved in management activities have an influence on resistance situations. Managers have a special responsibility in resistance situations simply because of their role. For this reason, it is managers who are particularly addressed in this book.

I have asked managers from smaller and larger companies to tell me about their everyday experiences of resistance. I will recount and explore these situations; this means, for example, asking new questions or assuming the perspective of the person or people the manager is talking about. My aim is to gain a better understanding of resistance by exploring the perspectives of all those involved and investigating how such challenging situations can be managed more productively. I do not want to lecture. Rather, I want to encourage readers to explore their own understanding of resistance and how to explore it in more detail and draw useful insights for their own practice.

The book illustrates various forms of resistance, some of which are to be expected, but some of which are quite surprising. This is followed by an examination of everyday explanations or what I call premature conclusions that stand in the way of a deeper exploration of resistance. I will then offer further possible explanations that also serve to improve our understanding of resistance. The book concludes with concrete tips for dealing productively with resistance.

# Overview: Chapters 1–7

Resistance is (almost always) an integral part of organizations and should not be blanked out, simply ignored, or kiboshed. Just as resistance in organizations should not be demonized, it should not be romanticized either. Resistance appears in all organizational relationships and is worth exploring. The book focuses on the following questions:

- How is resistance expressed and how does it arise?
- What is the reason for resistance or why is the behavior of organizational members described as "resistant"?
- How can management and those involved deal with resistance?

Chapters 2–4 are about making resistance tangible by describing in detail the various manifestations of resistance, as outlined above. In doing so, it becomes clear time and again that managers take certain mental shortcuts in resistance situations to explain the complex and demanding situations to themselves and remain capable of action. In Chapter 5, I work through these shortcuts or hasty conclusions that appear to clarify the situation but obscure a clear view of the resistance situation. Chapter 6 offers an in-depth look at the phenomenon of resistance. I present explanatory models that allow a more differentiated perception of resistance, but also provide information about the triggers of resistance and the dynamics of resistance situations. In the final chapter, Chapter 7, I draw conclusions for dealing with resistance. However, I not only talk about how managers can deal with it when they encounter resistance or when they perceive the behavior or statements of others as resistant, but also about the situation when they themselves create resistance. My aim is to shape resistance situations in such a way that they are an expression of appreciative management and leadership relationships and, if possible, lead to productive organizational dynamics.

Erik Nagel

# 1

# Resistance
## An Everyday Exception

It happens in life, as in grammar, that the exceptions
outnumber the rules.

—Rémy de Gourmont

I happen to be walking past Peter's office. I strike up a conversation with him about this and that. Peter works a lot from
home or directly at the customer's premises. The only thing on
his desk is his laptop. As is usual for him, there are no piles of
documents and no personal belongings in the room. For some,
the office probably exudes a pleasant sense of order, for others
an almost clinical cleanliness. In the middle of the conversation, I notice the leaflet about the Gamma project, which is
attached to the whiteboard right next to the doorway with two
oversized white magnets. Gamma is a major project that has triggered resistance within the organization. I am a member of the

strategic project committee and am therefore responsible for the project. I am aware that Peter is skeptical about it. I comment casually: "Was it you who put up the leaflet?" Peter looks at me with a smug smile and a steady gaze and replies: "Yes, I thought it was important for the management. So, of course, I just had to put it up." I can't help but smile and say that the management will certainly appreciate that.

I found the situation strange and a little uncomfortable. In my opinion, I have a good, trusting relationship with Peter. Humor and irony are simply part of our conversations. This situation was different in that he was noticeably critical of a project for which I was also responsible. It was no coincidence that he commented on the project to me in this way.

When this happened, I had already decided to write a book about resistance. However, I hadn't really delved into the subject matter. Was this resistance? And if so, then it had to be a particularly subtle form of resistance. In any case, this experience intensified my curiosity and motivated me to dig deeper into the topic of resistance and find out what is considered resistance and what forms it can take. While dealing with the topic, I gained an insight into the many ways resistance can manifest itself and why it arises in the first place. In the experience I described, resistance manifests in Peter's ironic comment. Even if the comment is formulated in a friendly and humorous way, Peter is expressing his criticism of the Gamma project. Is he challenging me, or does he just want to express his dissatisfaction? This and much more is unclear: Does he reject the project completely, is he ambivalent, or is his objection mainly directed against individual aspects of the project? Does he want to contribute critically or is he distancing himself? How can I deal with this type of resistance? Looking back on the experience, I realize I should have dug deeper because I never clarified what Peter's actual attitude or concerns were regarding the Gamma project.

In coaching sessions and when advising organizations, I have repeatedly found that dealing with resistance is a real challenge for managers. Likewise, as the episode above shows, I encounter resistance time and again in my own management and leadership practice. Sometimes it is a burden or irritating and remains a little mysterious because it cannot be immediately penetrated and understood. In my opinion, my observation and assessment of the diversity and relevance of the topic are not reflected in the standard textbooks. In most cases, resistance is seen as a negative side effect of change, or there is a call to take resistance seriously. However, these considerations do not usually go much deeper. I concluded that it is worth exploring resistance in more detail, as it plays such an important role in day-to-day management.

## 1.1 Managers Tell Their Stories

In this book, as already illustrated in the experience with Peter, managers themselves will have their say. They will tell stories about the specific situations in which they experienced, felt, or evoked resistance themselves. They report on what happened in detail, how they and the others involved in the situation behaved and how they categorize the experiences for themselves. Over 50 managers from Switzerland agreed to tell me their personal management stories about resistance. They were not asked to use an overthought definition of resistance, but rather how they use the term for themselves and what events they have experienced. The book therefore provides information on how the term "resistance" is dealt with in practice, in everyday work and management.

The managers entrusted me with their stories in the knowledge that I would use them for publications. I will initially recount the stories to illustrate a point, but then I won't automatically adopt the narrator's point of view. Instead, I will try to work out and reflect on the underlying assumptions. I take the narrators at their word and only refer to what they say when thinking about the situations described. In doing so, I will focus on the stage of everyday management life, but also dare to look behind the scenes of everyday experiences. On the one hand, I will try to shed light on the situation, but on the other I always ask myself how the actors and, above all, the managers could have grasped and handled the situation differently. I am aware that it is always easier to look at challenging resistance situations in hindsight. But I do this to do justice to all the people involved in the situation, to gain helpful insights and to present them in a way that the reader can understand. I hope that those managers who have described their cases to me will be able to understand my approach to their stories and take something away from them.

This is therefore not a book in which, as is often the case, events from high-profile major companies are reproduced. Rather, it is about the experiences of practitioners from normal larger and smaller organizations.

In addition to my own management experience and the research I have conducted myself and outlined above, many other researchers' work is included, supported by illustrative case studies. This should enable managers to reflect on their own practice and gain insights for their own management and leadership practice.

## 1.2  The Word "Resistance"

If the world of managers and their understanding of resistance are the primary focus of this book, then it cannot be a question of formulating a conclusive definition of resistance. Rather, it can be assumed that the word resistance is used or interpreted very differently depending on the context: Is a certain observed behavior identified as resistance at all? How is the observed behavior then evaluated?

Nevertheless, it makes sense to take a closer look at the origins of the word to understand its common uses and meanings today. The word resistance is a verbal noun meaning *the act or instance of resisting*. The verb resist means to oppose, withstand, refuse to accept, or refuse to comply with. Someone takes a stand against something or someone and may resist in a stubborn, tenacious, or even heroic way. From the opponent's point of view, the opposing person becomes an obstacle or hindrance.

Although the word resistance has found its way into organizational and management contexts as well as other disciplines such as psychology, in our everyday understanding we usually associate the word with mechanics, electrical engineering, and politics. In mechanics, resistance refers to a force that counteracts the movement of a body, and in electrical engineering it characterizes the property of certain substances that inhibits the flow of electric current. Or it refers to an electrical component that is used, for example, to limit electrical current to a certain value or to convert electrical energy into thermal energy. Resistance here is a normal, natural phenomenon, neither positive nor negative, which must be reduced or increased for certain purposes, and which fulfills a specific function.

However, the primary meaning of the word resistance is a political one. Here, resistance can be equated with a social state of emergency in which insurgents turn against those in power, especially if they use their influence against society or parts of it unscrupulously. The insurgents try to uncover the machinations or remove those in power. The Arab Spring comes to mind today as an example of resistance. Or we think of the several hundred students who blocked three main traffic arteries in the city center of Hong Kong for several weeks. But art and culture are also used in the fight against oppressive regimes: in 2012, for example, the punk rock group Pussy Riot staged a 41-second action in a Moscow cathedral. In doing so, they protested the alliance between church and state. Another example is the Chinese artist Ai Weiwei, who has been using art to fight against the Chinese regime for years.

The insurgents are fighting back against the unpredictable, powerful regimes and are doing so with great courage and sacrifice. They stand up for freedom, social justice, and a life of dignity and democracy. However, they also know that they cannot control the course of events. In the worst-case scenario, violence escalates, or authoritarian regimes take on a new guise. The insurgents and their supporters face greater dangers. They are harassed for years, and may be imprisoned, thus risking life and limb.

People are probably not always fully aware of the risks associated with acts of resistance, as the protests are carried out with tremendous conviction, euphoria, and strength. The Egyptian author Nagib Machfus, the son of the merchant family Jasin at the time of the British protectorate of Egypt, gave a vivid account of his experience. When the British prevented a delegation of Egyptian nationalists from attending the Paris Peace Conference in 1919, there were demonstrations and unrest. Jasin took part in one demonstration, got carried away, and completely forgot himself (Machfus 1996, p. 662):

> *Yes, it had been a wonderful day. The raging torrent had broken over him, and the unruly waves had swept him along like a thin, feather-light leaf, letting him glide along in whatever direction the current took. He could not believe that he had previously allowed himself to be guided only by reason and had followed events indifferently and uninvolved from a safe observation post. Fahmi's [Jasin's brother]*

*remark made him remember how he had marched in the demon-*
*stration, so that he, surprised at himself, was amazed: when you're*
*amongst so many people, you don't think about yourself at all. It's as*
*if you've become someone else.*

In this story, it becomes clear how political resistance allows those involved to ride an emotional wave. But outsiders are also emotionally gripped and intuitively take sides with the resisters if they represent the same values and concerns. The insurgents against authoritarian systems are the heroes of the day and they deserve full recognition, not only because we admire their courage, but also because we share their convictions.

In political resistance, all those involved are outside the regular course of events, and the existing order is often called into question, along with those who represent this order. Situations of political resistance therefore represent exceptional circumstances.

## 1.3 Resistance: Burden or Resource?

If we now look at the use of the word in specialist literature in the context of the management of organizations, the first thing we notice is that resistance, by contrast to political resistance, is usually addressed from the perspective of management. If we usually show solidarity with insurgents and view the situation from their perspective, this is reversed when we look at the context of the organization. Resistance then usually becomes a problem that management is confronted with. However, it is precisely this one-sided perspective that creates a difficulty in dealing with resistance. Taking the management's point of view means taking a position against those who stand in the way of management. Management is easily given a free pass: every-thing that comes from the top is then considered to be right, and there is no closer examination of the convictions on which management's actions are based and whether the resistance may (also) be justified.

Resistance is usually seen as a negative, disruptive, if not destructive side effect of controlled change that must be accepted or skillfully eliminated. In this logic, management arrives at a plausible and valid strategic decision which must be implemented after thorough analysis. If resistance then arises to the carefully considered decision from the management's point of view, it cannot be reasonable. The reaction to the management's decision is then quickly seen as tactical, as a defense of the past, or of one's own privileges and is directed against the future-oriented considerations of the management.

Experiencing resistance, especially when it is offensive and aggressive demands are made, is by no means a pleasant management experience. But this certainly does not justify a blanket negative assessment of resistance. As we will see in the book, this negative assessment of resistance is an almost automatic reflex of management or corporate governance. The question is whether this reflex does management and the organization a service – or rather a disservice?

For some time now, there have been calls for resistance to be seen not as a burden but as a resource, as it strengthens a culture of discussion, for example, or expresses a commitment on the part of employees (Ford et al. 2008, p. 368 et seq.). I fully agree with this perspective, but as a demand expressed in this form, it also remains strangely abstract and one-sided. Translated into everyday life, this view can quickly become a paradoxical challenge to managers: "Just look on the bright side." But how is a manager supposed to perceive a situation "simply in a positive light" if they are unable to take anything positive away from it? And it would also be misleading to view all resistance as positive – just as it would be misleading to view all management decisions as positive.

# 1.4 Resistance Is Part of Everyday Life

Another seemingly immutable truth about resistance is that it invariably arises as soon as change is involved. Change without resistance is inconceivable, as "people don't like change in principle," according to a frequently stated conviction. So, managers know that as soon as they set off and want to get the organization moving, things will get bumpy because there are deep potholes in the road and fog obscuring their view. To get through the journey in one piece, they need a few tools: an all-terrain SUV (project organization), a four-wheel drive (powerful promoters of the project), a navigation system (stringent management concept, planning with milestones and deadlines), impact protection, seatbelt, and airbag (thick skin) – and plenty of resolve (stamina and assertiveness). But why do we assume that the members of the organization will resist no matter what management does? I believe that such generalized assumptions do not really help us in resistance situations.

It is equally unconvincing or inaccurate to associate resistance solely with planned change. Smaller and larger, planned or unplanned changes are constantly occurring in organizations, so there are always situations for resistance to arise. It is much more likely that resistance occurs on different levels, sometimes visible and audible, sometimes subtle, and inconspicuous. Resistance is not limited to change. It appears – and this is described in detail in the book – in many different forms and is an extremely widespread phenomenon. In this respect, resistance is a priori neither positive nor negative; it is a completely *normal* part of everyday management and working life but is experienced as an *exceptional situation*.

When we think of resistance in organizations, we probably first think of strikes for higher wages or better working conditions or of dissatisfied employees resisting change processes.

However, resistance is often expressed in direct encounters with other members of the organization, as is clear from the stories told by managers. This overt resistance described in Chapter 2 is only part of the story. Resistance can also be hidden and only reveal itself as resistance at second glance. The issues involved in this form of resistance cannot be grasped as directly or addressed as immediately. I explore this hidden form of resistance in Chapter 3. This is followed by the question of whether resistance occurs in all organizations. As I show in Chapter 4, this is not the case. There are organizational conditions that lead to both overt and covert resistance being suppressed.

In presenting types of resistance, I do not claim to present all possible manifestations of resistance. It would probably also be presumptuous to claim to do so. Rather, I try to identify, present, and reflect on the most striking and important forms based on the stories of managers and broad research on the subject.

## 1.5 The Winds of Resistance Blow from All Directions

If it is assumed that resistance only occurs in change situations that are initiated by management or executives, then it is inevitably directed against the hierarchy and logically always comes from the employees. In this perception, they oppose the management and unnecessarily sabotage the strategically motivated, objectively legitimate project. Resistance is usually understood as resistance "from those down there" against "those up there." But it is not only the employees on the front line who are seen as a predestined hive of resistance. In 2008, Siemens CEO Peter Löscher announced mass redundancies to reduce the company's sales and administration costs by 10% within two years. It was not only the workers who were to make sacrifices, but – according to Löscher – it was now about "the layer of clay" (Löhr 2010). Let's interpret this metaphor a little: middle management is characterized quite sweepingly as an impermeable layer that continually blocks the decisions of top management. Middle management thus hinders the future development of the company and must therefore be dismantled. However, such an idea of organizational members unwilling to change first and foremost promotes a structural antagonism between employees or middle management and top management. This sounds suspiciously like an unavoidable, long-term battle between the management levels. If this were really the case, then in my opinion it would be the task of top management not to interpret this – especially not in a defamatory way – to justify a decision, but to do something to reduce such antagonism. Polemics and stigmatization are certainly not the right approach.

Managers experience resistance in completely normal, everyday management situations with their employees: during a spontaneous conversation in the manager's office, during a planned employee appraisal, or during a longer phase of reorganizing spheres of work. But it is far from the truth to assume that resistance only ever comes from below. In their descriptions throughout the book, managers make it clear that they also perceive resistance in their relationships with colleagues at the same management level. However, managers also perceive resistance in their relationships with superiors or top management. This can be seen, for example, in a study of a management development program at the car manufacturer Ford (Spreitzer, Quinn 1996). Over 3000 managers took part in this four-year program. They received sensitive strategic information that was normally reserved for top management. The aim was to create a sense of urgency and awareness of change at middle management level. The plan was to gradually transform the traditional functional structures into cross-functional teams and matrix structures.

In addition, the structural changes were to be accompanied by cultural developments. After an initial weekly program, the managers had six weeks to implement the changes. Whilst in some places middle managers implemented enormous and inconceivable optimizations after the training, such as the dramatic reduction of lead times, a small number of managers (1–2%) did not show up for the follow-up program. One middle manager explained this by saying, "Nobody really wants us to take the lead." This finding does not really fit in with the image we usually have of resistance. According to the perception of these managers, it is not the employees on the front line who are resisting, but the top management, the initiators of the change process themselves.

The winds of resistance blow from all directions, and it always seems to be a question of which direction it is coming from. In the book, I show that resistance is not an objective finding, but an interpretation. Interestingly, resistance is almost always attributed to others, and only in very rare cases is it acknowledged that resistance also comes from oneself.

## 1.6 The Zone of Uncertainty

When managers report on resistance situations, they are not just casual stories. They are usually experiences that are associated with strong emotions. A resistance situation has an unsettling and irritating effect. In some situations, it goes even further. Then the situation is perceived as a real threat to one's own position. Resistance situations don't really leave anyone cold, as they affect their own convictions and interests, which are questioned or ignored. Sometimes they are experienced as real turning points or changes of direction in the manager's own experience. As a manager, I am usually not a distanced observer, but I am or become involved in the situation, whether I want to or not. Experiencing or exercising resistance is therefore often perceived as very stressful. These are situations that are upsetting and have a lasting effect. They are certainly not situations that you actively seek out and desire. But they are part of everyday working and management life. So, experiences involving resistance are also episodes worth recounting because you are proud of them, questions remain unanswered, or you were or still are extremely upset about something.

Resistance situations are challenging, exceptional situations, in which schematic instructions are not really helpful. It is not always easy or clear how to deal with resistance. Managers are left to their own devices, having to reassess each situation and constantly find – or invent – their own appropriate approach to dealing with resistance. This book is intended to provide support with this.

In situations of resistance, the commonly accepted ideas of management, organization, and employees, but also very basic images of people, come to the fore or can be set in motion. Managers learn from situations of resistance, emerge stronger, or look back on the experience with irritation and, in some cases, resignation and bitterness. A closer look at resistance provides an insight into the diverse, contradictory, and tense microcosm of the organization. Many things become visible: promising paths that those involved can take, but also dead ends that those involved end up in with no way out in sight. In resistance situations, managers maneuver themselves into a *zone of uncertainty*, as they are surprised by the vehemence of the behavior, are unable to interpret the behavior, and do not always know exactly how to react. This book takes the reader directly into this zone of uncertainty. Certainties are called into question. That is the price of this journey. But this journey also holds great promise. Reading this book offers an in-depth understanding of incisive, stirring, and thoroughly entertaining experiences in organizations and thus offers new possibilities. Readers can reflect on their own attitudes and basic convictions, look at themselves and others in a different light, and ultimately develop their behavior. Resistance situations offer an opportunity to learn, but also to show management skills and increase strength for the good of the organization. Exploring resistance makes it possible to better recognize, understand, and classify situations. Resistance thus becomes more understandable and accessible. The aim of the book is to give managers a more comprehensive and differentiated picture of resistance and to show them ways of dealing with resistance productively.

However, we must not give ourselves false hope. Dealing with resistance is challenging and is not always pleasant. We should refrain from claiming to be able to fully understand all situations despite our education, knowledge, and experience. Some experiences remain impenetrably incomprehensible. This may be unsettling at first glance, but it can also have a relieving effect, as you don't always have to fully understand everything, and others feel the same way. It is much more important to have or develop the willingness, ability and, above all, curiosity to deal with situations of resistance in a different way. Resistance is also incredibly appealing. It is the salt in the soup. Because in situations of resistance, it is management, in the true sense of the word, that is required.

## Summary

- The aim of the book is to provide managers and all members of an organization with a more comprehensive and differentiated picture of resistance and thus to show ways in which resistance can be dealt with productively.

- On the one hand, resistance is normal (i.e. it is commonplace), and there are many opportunities in everyday life for resistance to arise and manifest itself. On the other hand, resistance is an exceptional situation, as particular resistance situations are perceived as stressful, irritating, and challenging to overcome.

- The book offers a very practical approach to resistance by reproducing the experiences of managers in the form of concrete management experiences, but also by reflecting on them in such a way that the readers can draw helpful conclusions for themselves.

- The book also contains extensive, very well illustrated and practice-relevant research on the topic. It thus offers a systematic and theoretically sound insight into the background to resistance and provides supportive tips for shaping resistance situations.

- In management theory, resistance is often seen as a negative side effect of change. Alternatively, resistance is seen as something positive. In this book, resistance is viewed as a phenomenon that is neither positive nor negative.

- Resistance can occur in all relationships. Put simply, it is not only employees who are experienced in evoking resistance, but also colleagues at the same management level or even superiors.

- A self-critical examination of resistance may be unsettling on the one hand, as certainties are called into question. On the other hand, this reflection also offers the reader the opportunity to understand resistance situations more comprehensively, to experience such situations in other ways, and to behave differently.

# Overt Resistance

He who fights, can lose. He who does not fight has already lost.
—Bertolt Brecht

Chapters 2–4 describe various instances of resistance. The first of these three chapters deals with overt resistance, which is clearly recognizable in everyday organizational and management life and is usually identified as resistance. In Chapter 3, we explore less obvious or covert forms of resistance. After all, there are also organizations in which resistance is strangely absent, does not appear, or is only a marginal phenomenon, which we deal with in Chapter 4.

Managers were asked to describe episodes that they *associate* with resistance. The resulting instances of resistance certainly have distinct similarities, but above all they reveal the diversity and complexity of how resistance is perceived and dealt with.

## 2.1 Resistance as an Emphatically Expressed Demand

When managers report episodes of resistance, they very often involve direct encounters and confrontations with employees, colleagues, or superiors. They are then confronted with unmistakable and emphatically expressed demands and are expected to take a stand and reach a decision. From the complainant's point of view, there is a risk of being met with a lack of understanding, being admonished or ostracized, or even losing their job. They wonder how the management will deal with their request or, more fundamentally, with the fact that a request has been made at all: is the complaint or demand being listened to and is an attempt being made to work out a solution together? Is it simply rejected as subjective or irrelevant? Is it considered an outrage to make a demand at all? Does the superior even feel offended? Or does the manager or management not see themselves as responsible and then delegate the problem back?

### Case Study: A Wage Dispute

A head of marketing in the food industry reported that the HR manager had asked the employees to think about possible wage claims for the coming year. The manager was then immediately confronted by an employee with a request for a massive pay rise. She reports further:

> *"I then prepared myself well for the year-end meeting with the employee. In other words, I obtained salary data for comparable positions with the same training and experience."*[1]

---

[1] These and all other case studies or stories from managers in this book have been linguistically edited, anonymized, and sanitized in such a way that they cannot be traced back to the organization or the individuals involved. I have made sure that the meaning of the statements made is preserved. If a story seems familiar or well known, it can be assumed that it is not about the experiences of a person known to the reader, but rather a typical experience with resistance.

When preparing for the second employee appraisal, the head of marketing discovered that there were some massive wage differences in her area, but that she did not have much latitude for wage adjustments due to the budget. From the manager's point of view, however, the employee was a very good worker whom she was keen to retain. Another meeting was held:

> *"At the year-end meeting, the demand was then repeated unequivocally, and reference was made to other jobs in the market where this wage could be achieved. I was then able to agree with the employee that a wage increase of this magnitude in one step was impossible, but that wage development to this level was certainly possible over several years. In the first step, I was able to make an extraordinary pay rise possible, and in the following years I adjusted the salary slightly above average each year. In this way, I was able to motivate the employee and compensate for the wage differences in the area within the scope of my budget."*

The manager initially identifies resistance on the part of the employee due to the initially surprising, seemingly excessive, wage demand. However, she immediately takes the expressed concern seriously and begins to investigate further. This leads to new insights: apparently there are irregularities which have been caused by the organization. The initially very high wage claim appears in a new light and therefore appropriate, or more appropriate. The manager takes responsibility for the irregularities caused by the organization and involves the employee in the discovery process by explaining the background to their decision in detail. This lays the foundation for a solution that is acceptable to both sides, even if the employee's request cannot be fully and immediately met. The solution is based on a serious discussion between the manager and the employee. The employee is involved in the decision-making process in so far as he is given transparent information about the manager's maneuverability. However, the situation also succeeds due to the employee's willingness to acknowledge the framework conditions presented and the efforts of the manager to find a good solution for him.

## Case Study: A Disgruntled Employee

Not all situations end so smoothly, of course. A head of a procurement business unit, also from a food company, reports on how the resistance of one person led to their dismissal. The head of a business unit and the head of the logistics department assigned to him were each looking for a commercially trained person to support them. One person would take on the role of support for the head of the business unit and another person would provide support for the head of logistics. The position of support for the head of the business unit was the line manager for the position of support for the head of department. Many applicants were interested in the line manager position. This position was also better paid. The head of the business unit opted for a person he already knew, Nadine. He forwarded the other applications to the head of logistics, who then chose Jeannine Huber for the second vacancy. Jeannine Huber was between jobs at the time and was able to start work immediately. Nadine Fischer was still tied to her previous employer and was only able to start four and a half months later. The head of the business unit reports further:

> *"During this transition phase, Jeannine Huber had to take over some of Nadine Fischer's work and help out. However, this was explained to her before she took up the position. Ms. Huber then got to grips with the job very quickly and well. She did a good job. However, we soon noticed that Ms. Huber had some personal issues and was very unbalanced as a result. But when Ms. Fischer took up the position, Ms. Huber no longer wanted to hand over the work and no longer*

*wanted to do her proposed job because, according to her own state-*
*ment, she had proved in recent months that she was capable of much*
*more and therefore wanted a different job. This went so far that she*
*refused to work for her boss. We eventually had to part ways with*
*Ms. Huber because she was also unwilling to work with her line*
*manager, Ms. Fischer. Although we told Ms. Huber from the outset*
*what the next steps would be, she reacted to the planned change with*
*great resistance. Today, of course, we ask ourselves what we could have*
*done better."*

From the management's point of view, Jeannine Huber had
put up resistance. The employee makes it unmistakably clear that
she has a right to the more demanding and higher-paid position, as she has proven that she is up to the task. In this case,
the line manager does not comply with the employee's request.
This is because her demand contradicts the arrangement agreed
at the beginning and she also refuses to cooperate. An untenable
situation. The employee is dismissed.

Who is responsible for the unfavorable outcome in this situation? At first glance and from the managers' point of view, it
is the defiant and belligerent employee, who also appears to
have personal issues. But in the end, the managers reflect on
whether they could have behaved differently. The events can
certainly be interpreted differently: was the agreement beyond
doubt and could not the managers have foreseen the situation? Is
the employee's reaction not also understandable, that she wants
to take on a task that matches her proven abilities? Suddenly
the cause of the resistance is no longer so clear. Is the cause of the
unfortunate outcome of the episode to be sought in the employee
with significant deficits or is the cause to be found in the management's approach and is it therefore a management error? In
the case of a management error, the management would have to
be responsible or jointly responsible for the fact that resistance
was put up in the first place.

Now let us look at the agreement again: the offer is probably attractive for the employee because she can then review for a limited period whether she is up to the job. Rejecting the agreement proposed by her superiors right at the beginning of her employment would also be sensitive for the employee, as the superiors could have interpreted this as a refusal and doubts could have arisen about the employee's commitment. The case description also states that Jeannine Huber "was obliged to" take on the work. It can be assumed that she had no choice. So how level was the playing field here? After the first phase of successful induction, the employee "was then obliged to" permanently take on a task that, from her point of view and at this later point in time, was below her ability level. In addition, her superiors had also confirmed shortly beforehand that she had done a "good job." She now sees herself forced to perform a permanent job that is below her abilities. The employee probably feels that this is an unjustified demotion. Even if her reaction did not necessarily have to be like this, it is still in no way unjustified behavior. The cause of the resistance then no longer lies with the employee, who according to this view is making a perfectly understandable demand but lies in the agreement. And this agreement was initiated and decided by management to solve a problem for themselves or the organization. The management should have been aware that the agreement could be problematic.

However, when looking at this case and all the other cases in this book, it is not about pointing the finger at someone and looking for the "real culprit." It is not primarily about the question of what the management could have done differently, but rather about making it clear what part the respective parties involved played in an unfortunate situation. In this way, management can acknowledge its part and take responsibility. In relation to the specific case, this means that the management takes responsibility for the employee's problem caused by the agreement.

It would have been best for the management to look for solutions together with Jeannine instead of blaming her for the problem. Whether she would then have cooperated and the case would have ended better is speculation. At the very least, the management would have assumed its responsibility.

## Case Study: A Hierarchical Dispute

Of course, managers also experience that their own demands are not heard or cannot be implemented. A manager from the transport industry gives an account from her organization. Within the division relevant to this case study, there are three departments (the northern, southern, and western sales regions), which in turn are divided into areas. The manager reporting here is an area manager in the western sales region. A vacancy has arisen in the northern sales region:

> *"The head of the northern sales region asked two members of my team of four behind our backs whether they would like to take up the vacant positions. As this was a promotion for both, they agreed after a short time. Both were the driving force behind my team. During a break in a management meeting, the head of the northern sales region informed my boss, the head of the western sales region, and me of the choice. Our first reaction: surprise and silence."*

On the way home, the head of the western sales region and the area manager exchanged views and identified the problems they were facing. They were annoyed by the way employees were being poached behind their backs. They then decided to raise this issue at the next meeting with the divisional manager and vehemently oppose the selection. For the meeting a few weeks later, they "armed" themselves with arguments to explain to the divisional manager the gap that could not be filled. They assumed that they would receive backing from the divisional manager for their opposition to this planned selection. The meeting began:

*"When this business came up according to the agenda, we were very surprised that the divisional manager had already been informed in detail and told us that this had been done with his approval: 'The best people must be selected for the appropriate positions.' Of course, we tried to present our arguments and problems. However, we soon realized that although they would be heard, this would not change the decision. Resigned to fate, we gave up our resistance and realized that the two employees would be leaving us in three months' time. It was then that I realized that the story had been cleverly orchestrated by the head of the northern sales region and that everything had already been decided by the time we heard about it. I was very disappointed with the way the decision was made. The discussion about it was pointless from the outset. I also clearly missed the overall view behind this decision. Although the problem of the northern sales region was solved, we now had a huge problem that we had to solve ourselves."*

The fears that had been expressed then actually materialized. And three years later, the team was still suffering the effects of the abrupt vacancy. In addition, there was increased fluctuation in the department team. That's the story so far.

From the point of view of the area manager and the head of the western sales region, the head of the northern sales region is acting purely tactically and succeeds in getting the divisional manager on his side. They feel they are being deceived and do not receive any support for their concerns. From their point of view, the head of the northern sales region should have been put in his place and the divisional manager should not have allowed himself to be instrumentalized. If we follow the story, the head of the northern sales region and the divisional manager have played a dirty game. The divisional manager has a responsibility to ensure clean, fair, and comprehensible decision-making processes, which he did not do in this case.

Next, let us look at the role of the area manager and her line manager. Their demand is clear. Their aim is to reverse the decision. However, it is also clear from what has been said that the poor quality of the decision-making process is directly linked to the decision itself and the opponent: the tactically skillful, if not scheming, person who sets up an underhanded decision-making process, resulting in a decision that only benefits the mastermind and leaves the western sales region as the aggrieved party. The perception is that the underhandedness of the procedure cannot lead to a justified decision. This makes it clear that the assessment of the problematic decision-making process outweighs the material decision. From the point of view of the area manager and the head of the western sales region, the decision is wrong because the decision-making process faltered. The narrative does not consider the possibility that the decision could have been right, even though the decision-making process was wrong.

What happens next in the case? The managers plan the resistance and want to fight the decision. However, they then abandon their plan after they fail to achieve their goal of reversing the decision. Negative emotions overwhelm them. Their disappointment at the unfair decision-making process weakens their resistance. They become victims of the power play and resign.

It did not necessarily have to end like this. Let us separate the decision-making process from the decision. The criticism from the area manager and the head of the western sales region that they were not involved in the decision-making process as responsible persons is very understandable. No question about it. But this does not mean that the decision to give capable employees the opportunity to develop within the company is absurd. On the contrary, it would probably have been highly demotivating for those employees who were offered the development step if their direct superiors had prevented them from taking up an attractive opportunity per se. The employees would then probably have judged this decision-making process as wrong. The area team would probably have stayed together but would have fallen apart.

Questionable decision-making processes do not automatically produce questionable decisions, which in turn of course does not justify questionable decision-making processes. The area manager and the head of the western sales region could have acknowledged the decision, but then worked hard to ensure that they received the same support in solving their newly created problem. Instead of giving up resistance and giving free rein to negative emotions, they could have continued to focus on their concerns and defended them with full conviction and persistence. Those who made the unwelcome but entirely understandable decision, albeit unfairly, could have been reminded of their responsibility for the consequences of the decision and could have assumed this responsibility. In addition, the area manager and the head of the western sales region could have worked to ensure that they were involved in such decision-making processes in the future.

## Case Study: An Insensitive Approach

In the previous cases, it is always a matter of personnel and directly job-related issues. However, demands can also be considered in a completely different context, namely when it comes to changes in the entire organization. In the following case (Courpasson et al. 2012), two things are striking: managers and not employees put up resistance, and the resistance is not directed against change, but triggers change. Specifically, it concerns a French bank where the supervisory board decided to blacklist two relatively small branches located in rural areas. Two managers had been running these branches for over 15 years and stood for a culture of customer proximity, which came under fire because of the new banking policy. The reason for the resistance was that the marketing department sent a notice to all 24 branches classifying the various branches. The criteria used included the number of products sold in the last three months. The memo emphasized the shortcomings of the two smaller branches and demanded explanations for the poor performance. Max was considered one of the most successful branch managers and was furious with the management:

> *"They spent time in meetings talking about trust and commitment and cooperation and friendship, and the power of the 'Household' (the company). And all of a sudden, wham, a cold note identifying two branches ..."*

In Max's opinion, the management's approach contradicted the bank's culture. On the one hand, the bank's results were typically seen as a collective achievement and not as the sum of the individual performances of the branches. And when problems arose, they were solved informally:

> *"If there is a problem somewhere, we talk about it ... yeah, that's a culture of sharing things, we do not really compete with each other; we strive to find germane places for everybody."*

Max was regarded as a very good, loyal employee and in no way a rebel. The company was not his whole world, but he owed a lot to the bank, which had hired him 10 years ago at the age of 28. He was aware that the bank had hired new experts in the last two years to implement new service regulations. Max quickly understood that tension was brewing between two business cultures. He decided to act because he felt it was "ethically unfair" and "overly political" to brand two specific branches as underperforming. Max initiated a resistance group. He invited six colleagues with whom he felt a personal connection. Some of them managed the best-performing branches. After a few days and discussions on the phone, the group met for two 3-hour sessions and agreed on the content of the complaint and that it needed to be initiated quickly to avoid further new rules. Above all, the group saw a danger that the balance of power could shift from the branches to the marketing department and that the marketing people would impose their views on the whole bank. In terms of content, they quickly agreed that the same performance criteria could not be used for all branches. The seven group members wrote a 15-page statement, signed it in alphabetical order, and sent it directly to the CEO.

With their approach, the branch managers went directly to the CEO and the board of directors, bypassing the section heads (i.e. the management level above them). They were convinced that they did not need the hierarchy to lend credibility to their demands. This approach made the resistance official and gave them the feeling that they could make a difference. Frank, one of the rebelling branch managers, said that they had:

> *"the feeling of being, say, powerful, of having the right to say no and to explain why and to suggest ways to move forward."*

In the report, they mentioned that they did not agree with the type of communication in the form of an impersonal, formal message:

> *"The initial note sounds authoritarian and strives to impose new criteria without having even discussed the issue with us. This is not acceptable."*

They also suggested discussing the "very important topic of branches' performance criteria" with the management board. They also threatened consequences if no discussion took place. They stated that in such a case, the gang of seven would suspend the annual appraisal of its branch employees. It was clear to the group that the top management's reaction was far from predictable, as the behavior was simply "outrageous" at first glance.

The report reached the CEO at an awkward time, as larger banks were examining the company with a view to a takeover.

He wanted to avoid unrest at all costs. At first glance, he felt "embarrassed" by the report, but he concluded that he had to act quickly. He sent the report to the other board members. He knew his people and knew that the resistance did not just happen on a whim:

> "I (…) knew they made it a fundamental issue between them and the marketing director and staff. I did not want to encourage that, but I understood that it was serious … We couldn't carry on as if nothing had happened."

He was looking for a way to reduce internal tensions and save face. He called Max, making it clear that he assumed Max had triggered the process, and arranged an initial meeting for the following week, which would include the marketing director. The CEO tried to initiate a dialog between the opposing stakeholder groups and decided to set up a working group with seven representatives from the branches and three people from the marketing department. Max was put in charge of the working group, and another branch manager from the rebel group also took part. The marketing director, who was also invited, declined to attend the first meeting and sent a deputy. The working group met seven times and developed new criteria that considered the context of the branches and the principle of fairness to assess the contributions of the branches. The 30-page report written by Max was discussed several times by the board members and the section heads. The working group succeeded in developing specific criteria to overcome the economic difficulties experienced by the local branches. By contrast, the previous approach of the marketing experts only aimed to evaluate the practices of the branches in a standardized way.

In retrospect, the CEO indicated that he was convinced by the demands of the resistance group. He did not have the impression that certain branches were underperforming, and he also saw the cultural problem that had arisen. And he interpreted Max's initiative and the formation of the resistance group as an expression of identification with the bank and the bank's specific cultural characteristics: taking initiative, making autonomous decisions, and being concerned about the bank. In addition, Max was "simply the best" from the CEO's point of view. The marketing director, on the other hand, was simply "too radical," refusing to "take a step back and talk":

> *"I guess he was afraid of talking business with Max, and he thought I was on Max's side. Maybe he was right. But he misinterpreted my decision that led to the eventual task force."*

The marketing manager had a completely different explanation for the events:

> *"That's not a thing we are used to, people contesting something not contestable. The fact was that a couple of branches were strikingly underperforming, and we wanted explanations from the managers. And they said no, and the boss was afraid of, I don't know, a strike or something. Moreover, the contest was led by a pretty influential guy, and the boss was not ready to have a fight with him. He was the kind of super-performing guy, the example in meetings, the highest bonuses on the charts, blah, blah, blah. (...) It was unbelievable that their demands got such a welcoming answer ... And there was this terrible task force to design and implement supposed new rules for assessing branches' performance and so forth. Task force convened, I don't know, something like 10 times in three months, to back up those dissenters and make a set of propositions because they were sort of experts. Obviously. And the new rules, as the boss said, were supposed to help the firm to better supervise local business, provide better control over the business, and blah, blah, blah. But it was all about reinforcing the power of these branch guys. I decided to leave some weeks later as the result of the task force denigrating what I strove to implement in my two years as the bank's marketing manager."*

This incident should first be examined more closely from the perspective of the three groups of actors: the resistance group behaves actively and forms themselves into a group whose members are top performers at the bank who are not suspected of simply showing solidarity with the weak and opposing the management on principle. They are aware of their high level of legitimacy and gain great self-confidence from this, but they are also taking a risk with their brazen approach and threats. They decide to raise a rational objection by acknowledging the management's fundamental concern on the one hand, but on the other hand by explaining in detail why they reject its implementation. With the well-founded report, they enter the "forbidden zone" (i.e. the top management's sphere of influence and responsibility). With the demands formulated in the report, they make their resistance public. They challenge management by questioning decisions that have already been presented as a fait accompli.

The danger here is that the CEO and top management feel exposed and discredited. They are not demanding a specific solution but show willingness to engage in dialog. By threatening, they signal that they are serious, but also increase their own risk. Once their demand has been met, they become involved in the search for new solutions. The ability of the resisters to present their complaint and their reputation are decisive factors in ensuring that the resistance is tolerated and accepted. At first, the CEO feels duped, as the vehemently voiced opposition is tantamount to mutiny at first glance. However, he quickly recognizes that the factual and cultural considerations are fundamentally justified, without explicitly revealing his sympathy for them. Rather, his primary concern is an overriding one. He wants to settle the dispute. The special feature of this approach is that the usual hierarchy is temporarily suspended for this issue to play out. A dialog takes place at eye level. This is triggered or invoked by the resistance group, but then facilitated by the CEO. This process allows the approach and therefore an important feature of the bank's policy to be reworked in a cooperative manner. The CEO does not simply let things happen passively but leads the process by setting up a working group and organizing discussions at various levels. Finally, the marketing director refuses to engage in the discussion, as he considers the contradiction in substance and form to be illegitimate and sees a conspiracy behind it, which was already decided to his disadvantage from the outset due to the strength of the top rebel and the weakness of the CEO. For him, it is a mere power play. He feels belittled, discredited, and robbed of the fruits of his two years of work.

The resistance in this case study is the cause of the change that is taking place. A company-wide dialog is getting under way and, it seems, is also generating good results. However, there are also downsides, as not all stakeholders see this process as productive and consensual. Two fundamental perspectives clash and remain incompatible: on the one hand, the dialog orientation, in which the participants, who are normally in hierarchical management relationships, are at eye level for a limited period of time. On the other hand, the hierarchy orientation does not tolerate a softening of the hierarchical power relationship at any time. From the perspective of the hierarchy orientation, the process appears to be an unbecoming and unfair power struggle and produces a victim.

But it could also be that the entire marketing department sees itself as the loser. That did not necessarily have to happen. One could have assumed that the recruitment of new experts and their task of issuing new service regulations amounted to a cultural conflict. The management process had therefore been designed to impose new rules for some time, and given the existing culture, the conflict was foreseeable. The marketing director (against the backdrop of his corresponding understanding of management) simply implements the regulation mandate and thus becomes the victim of a management omission. However, his contribution to the problem cannot be ignored – he could have familiarized himself with the bank's culture and implemented the process for developing new service regulations with the involvement of the key stakeholder groups. As it is, he ran blindly into the immediately escalating conflict. In the situation itself, he could only see the CEO's proposed course of action as humiliating from his own perspective. Without having any further knowledge of the case, the question arises as to whether the management made sufficient efforts to align the views and perspectives of all stakeholders in good time.

## 2.2 Resistance as an Open and Endless Power Struggle

The marketing manager's perspective in the section above already points to another manifestation of resistance: the kind of resistance which arises from a power struggle. The actors are constantly asking themselves questions such as the following: How do you keep the upper hand? How can you keep the other person down or bring them even lower? How can you reduce the other person's sphere of influence to increase your own? How can I outsmart the other person? How can I defeat him or her? What is the other person planning to do to curtail my influence? How can I use others for my own purposes to achieve my goal?

In power struggle mode, you are constantly on your guard, sensing underhand moves and not trusting your opponent. If you do not act in this way yourself, you may lose out and have to leave the field defeated. Power must be countered by means of strength and tactics, which can lead to a grueling spiral of conflict and struggle. It is hard to imagine a way out of a seemingly endless power struggle because that would require trust and openness. But if the first signals of trust are transmitted, this could be abused by the other party.

In this section, we look at two illustrative examples of open power struggles. In both cases, the resistance comes from the other side. The first case is about a relationship between two management colleagues and the second about a long-term change process. Both cases show how energy-draining this resistance can be, but also how those involved become entangled in hopeless power games.

## Case Study: A Power Play

A head of procurement from the electricity industry, Regula, reports on a rivalry with her colleague Urs, the head of the IT department. Regula realizes that Urs is resisting her, and a power struggle ensues. She recognizes that she is also contributing to this power play. They are mutually spiteful and distrusting. She describes the relationship as follows:

> *"I can actually have constructive discussions with all my colleagues at the second management level and implement joint projects, except for one colleague, the Head of IT. We regularly get into each other's hair and this can be poisonous. I don't trust him. I have the feeling that he is not competent, that he defends what he has, and is afraid of losing power and having to make concessions."*

From Regula's point of view, a consolidation of IT tasks at group level was foreseeable in the company. Two projects were launched, firstly the evaluation of group procurement (in the narrator's area of responsibility) and secondly the introduction of a joint telephone platform (in the other party's area of responsibility). Regula was asked by the CIO of the group whether she could support the telephone project from a procurement perspective. She agreed because she was interested in the topic and the CIO had confidence in her. In her own words, this enabled her to finally gain an insight into the IT activities at the group.

Urs also sat on the project committee. Regula describes how he vehemently opposed her participation:

> *"He complained to me vehemently about what I was doing getting involved in an IT issue. In my view, once again a power issue. We will have massive earnings problems in the next two years and have to start looking at costs from the group perspective. I can't understand why he doesn't realize what's going to happen here on a large scale. He now accuses me of only looking at things from a group perspective and no longer looking at my own company. I perceive a limited view in him, a preservationist attitude instead of a forward-looking, constructive, and creative attitude. I can't yet predict what disputes I will get into with him. But I will definitely work to benefit everyone."*

From the point of view of the narrating manager, the opponent's resistance manifests itself in two ways. Urs is resisting a completely obvious, unavoidable development and is resisting it because he sees her as the driver or symbol of this development. And the resister only does this because he feels directly threatened in his position. The explanations are carefully chosen ("I have the feeling") and yet she sees herself as arguing objectively and rationally, whereas her opponent is unobjective and irrational. The narrator sees herself as competent, has her eye on the big picture, and claims to be shaping the foreseeable future with great foresight and curiosity. She perceives her opponent as incompetent, who is only interested in preserving his own sphere of power and responsibility, and who tries to defend the status quo by any means necessary. The cause of the rivalry is in his resistance to the inevitable development. The attacks must be parried with counterattacks in order to retain the upper hand in this destructive game. Both drive the game of rivalry and become entangled in an unbecoming battle from which there is no escape.

If we look at the vehemence of the conflict, it is difficult to imagine how the two opponents can get out of this rivalry dynamic on their own. Deep mistrust characterizes this relationship. Once the engine of rivalry has been started, it is difficult to turn it off again. At this point, the people involved experience the relationship purely from a power perspective and deny any factual legitimacy to each other's arguments. The objective discussion about the necessity and meaningfulness of centralization and decentralization is no longer conducted at all, as the parties involved hold opposing positions. This conflict puts a strain on the relationship between the opposing parties, will also be visible to others, and will have an impact on them.

A clarification process could be demanded by superiors at this point, justified by the fact that the destructive conflict has a negative impact on the direct cooperation between the two people, and on the working atmosphere in the environment. A "curative intervention" would explore:

> *"which points of conflict are present and how they are experienced, what mutual conditioning and wounds have already arisen in the course of the conflict, etc. The interventions can then be directed at these points. The interventions can then focus on this in order to create a relaxed state in which the former parties to the conflict can work together constructively again"* (Glasl 2013, p. 316 et seq.).

Tensions can be reduced through de-escalating procedures. However, it may also be appropriate to choose escalating interventions to make it clear how unbearable the conflict actually is for those directly involved and the environment, so that the parties then feel motivated to engage in real conflict resolution (Glasl 2013).

## Case Study: An Overzealous Reorganization

Open and blunt resistance is often associated with change processes, as previously mentioned. It is often assumed that resistance cannot be avoided anyway. In the following, a departmental secretary of a Swiss cantonal administration describes his experiences with resistance to a change project for which he himself is jointly responsible. He reports on a long-term process that was initiated in an ivory tower and then implemented in the face of massive resistance that repeatedly flared up. The basic idea was to place three municipal organizational units with inter-municipal tasks under the responsibility of the canton. This meant that 700 employees were no longer employees of the borough, but of the canton. As part of this decision, it was also decided that there would have to be completely new structures to simplify management and save costs. The department secretary, who was still a controller in the project group at the beginning, reflects on the approach at the start of the change process:

> "We simply wanted to bring it together. Just one boss for all organizational units and no longer three bosses. That was a development process in the minds of us bureaucrats or technocrats. We sat down together and said: 'This is what we're going to do and then we'll move all the areas of activity and combine them more ideally.' It's really interesting when you can operate in a green field with organizations like this. We mainly thought about the areas of activity and the organizations, which have to function efficiently. We never thought about the people, or only rarely. We simply said: 'We have to inform them and so on and so forth.'"

A self-criticism of the approach can be heard in the narrative. The organization is seen as a (dys)functional, technical structure and not as a living entity that is brought to life by people with stories, expectations, and values. The management and project group were concerned with building a simpler, logical, and efficient organization. The finished solution was then presented to the 700 employees. Resistance quickly arose in all three organizational units. The planned reorganization affected regional political interests, so that politicians immediately became involved, and the resistance was felt on a larger scale.

The project group began to think tactically about how it could win over the politicians. The first commission meeting was held with the politicians:

> *"The head of the office came up with huge plans and said: 'To make it efficient, we have to do it this way and that way.' When it comes to efficiency, a politician first tries not to say anything against it. It was only over the course of the two-hour meeting that the regional representatives became more and more powerful toward us. They had objections such as: 'Despite all the efficiency – we can't lose this area in our region.'"*

The outcome of the meeting was sobering:

> *"In the end, everything was watered down. At the beginning, we came up with plans that were totally fine, and in the end, we went out with ten different variants because the politicians reared up on their hind legs."*

The head of the office fought like a lion against the increasing dilution of the substance of the reorganization, but also saw the creative aspects of the new structure increasingly dwindle. The project group became increasingly frustrated in a long and arduous six-month negotiation process, as the new solution deviated completely from the original plans over time. However, the project managers relentlessly stuck to their organizational idea of forming a structural unit with three locations. Over time, the structural solution became "their anchor." They held on to it so as not to become too frustrated. They were prepared to make concessions to the politicians when it came to "shifting fields of activity" so that the "politicians would calm down." But they were not prepared to give up the uniform management structure.

After the dispute with the politicians seemed to have been resolved, the organizational units suddenly made their presence felt. The new managing director of the merged organizational unit was elected by the department, then later replaced, a new one was elected, also replaced, and so on. Some good people were simply "thrown to the wolves." The flames of resistance flared up in one place, died out and then flared up again in the same or a different place. Sometimes the resistance came from the organizations, then again from politicians.

The newly installed managers polished the surface a little and left everything as it was or tried hard but failed. Or they received the order from the head of the department to "give it a thorough cleaning." Many people "fell off the wagon." The reorganization led to a years-long battle, which sometimes erupted into a slanging match, such as at an internal information event on the change process, at which the department secretary gave a presentation:

> *"There was shouting from the audience of a hundred people. You're there in front. And you're being personally shot at about what a half-wit you are for saying this and that, because this and that isn't true. You're reproached in front of a hundred people from a completely micro perspective. Played straight at the man."*

The manager describes a rather relaxed approach to this confrontational situation:

> *"I already knew a bit about it from another big project. That might also have something to do with age. I have the ability to distance myself or to distance myself from certain things that I say. And that specifically – it didn't really bother me. At most, it would have been a problem if I had been dragged around in the newspaper. But that was never the case with me. It was much worse with the head of department. He wasn't well at all for a while. Exactly for that reason."*

It was only after a long time, after a few years, that the realization dawned that things could not go on like this. The department secretary informed his colleagues in the project management team that "you can't fire everyone, after all." He initiated a broad-based project and involved all key personnel. Twenty people formulated a project assignment. However, there was no question of it becoming "an institution." Discussions about the project brief went on for six months, with those involved struggling over every word. Then the implementation phase began, which was moderated by an external consultant. But the project failed:

> *"The moderator tried to get the whole thing together with them so that we at least had a concept of how we could position ourselves. The various fronts then virtually paralyzed each other. Despite the moderation, despite the relatively broad involvement. It was too broad. The mistrust was too great."*

At the very beginning of the change project, the current department secretary was certain that he was on the right track and was convinced that he had to fight for an overarching, substantiated objective. But the resistance was persistent and seemed increasingly insurmountable. The organization simply could not rest. He no longer blamed the resistant employees for the ongoing, unproductive dynamics, but to the initiators and those responsible for the change process, including himself. Old certainties about "backward" or "oversensitive" employees and blaming others dissolved and after all these years, the department secretary is now faced with new, unanswered questions:

> *"My opinion has changed quite a lot in these seven years. In the beginning, I thought: 'Why are they so whiny now? Don't be so sensitive now; we have to reorganize too! We can save money here!' I had the same relatively hard line from the head of department, and I took the same line. Later I thought: 'That can't be right. We're doing something wrong. It can't be that it's breaking out like this again everywhere.' I then mainly directed it at us – at our inability to satisfy*

*these people with their injuries. Sitting at the table with them. Why didn't we manage to do that? Where exactly is the damage? Why can't I understand it? (...) From today's perspective, with all that we have learned? We went about it all wrong. We underestimated the regional cultures and structures."*

A culture of mistrust and opposition had become firmly established and resistance would – according to the department secretary's assumption – break out again and again in the future:

*"If we put a concrete shell around it now, like in Chernobyl, it will pop up again in another place. That's the crazy thing."*

This insight at the end of the manager's story is directly linked to his own change of role. At the beginning, he sees the change project from his role as (efficiency optimizing) controller. In his role as departmental secretary, he then no longer sees himself as responsible only for a functional logic (saving money), but also for the overall result (success/failure), because he can also be held responsible for this:

*"Of course, I also have a certain responsibility, as I was there from the very beginning. In the past, as Head of Finance, I would have said: 'I'm all about the money.' But in my role as department secretary, it was clear to me that we had to bring it to a favorable end."*

The responsibility is expressed that he stands by his insight and vehemently defends it at management level. He declares the previous practice to be unsuccessful, exposing and problematizing the images of humanity on which this practice is based. He also sets conditions for the project management committee, thereby emphasizing his point of view.

*"The last time it broke out like this again, I said: 'Now I just don't want to keep my mouth shut anymore. I don't want to allow another head of department or others to come and tell us to shoot people.*

*That's not possible. I don't want to. If our people are doing it so stupidly and we've been doing it for ages, then we need to rethink our approach and stop playing hardliner. Otherwise, I won't take responsibility for anything.' That's what I said in this room. Then they listened to me. I want to bring it to a favorable end."*

This reconsideration leads him to the conclusion that the change should not have been implemented as a solution devised by the hierarchy, but as a carefully and prudently designed participation process. The project management should have had sufficient time to analyze the situation properly at the beginning and develop a procedural concept with various key figures from the organizational units. The organizational solution, which was developed at the beginning of the change process by a small group at the top of the organization, maintained against all resistance, and whose implementation was used as the sole indicator of the success of the change, would have to be abandoned – honestly and authentically. The sacred cow would have to be slaughtered. This is the insight of the departmental secretary. In his opinion, open questions evaluating previous experiences should be prioritized over new answers and solutions:

*"There is a study from the beginning of the process. It says that from an organizational and technical point of view, it is not good to run the organizational units with just one boss and three locations: 'Why don't you stick to what you had before and work a little more closely together?' That should have made us a little more aware of how we should have proceeded in this process. We didn't even realize that. We were so far away and thought: 'Yes, what are they doing now?' The way they're doing it now is nonsense. But for them, it's such an important part of their culture. We completely underestimated it."*

*"I'd even go so far as to talk about the organization. About the: 'Three locations, one institution.' We take this study again and ask ourselves: 'What is good and what is bad here? How could we still achieve the objective together?' That's it."*

What is remarkable about this story is how long the management stuck to its principles and tried to push through its solutions despite resistance from the organization. Against the background of the image of humanity, which leads to resistance not really being taken seriously, and the understanding of change outlined above, the management's adherence to its own paradigms is very understandable. The convictions became deeply ingrained in the self-image and were continuously confirmed, also through mutual assurances. The remarkable thing is that over time, the narrator begins to doubt whether the assumptions of the management were and are the right ones. Over time, he experiences a never-ending resistance and, motivated by a sense of responsibility for the failure, realizes that the real problem is not the resistance, but the project managers' understanding and practice of change. Over time, the narrator succeeds in distancing himself from the existing change processes. He problematizes what was previously considered undisputed and puts himself in the position of the members of the organization. In doing so, he recognizes which problematic ideas he and the management committee have held on to for years and which they no longer question. And he now formulates what could be important to the others (i.e. the members of the organization).

"I can't get rid of the ghosts I summoned." This is one way to explain the manager's realization process. The unpredictable and unrelenting resistance is no longer simply interpreted as the annoying behavior of unreasonable people. Resistance is linked to the design of the change process and not just seen as a detached phenomenon. The realization is not an easy one, because suddenly he is also, or even largely, responsible for the fact that others have shown resistance and continue to do so to this day.

## 2.3  Resistance as Whistleblowing

Whistleblowing is also overt resistance, where one person turns against the whole organization and fights against it. Anyone who blows the whistle on an organization can become a hero (to the public) and at the same time a traitor (to the organization). The act usually attracts public attention. This can be judged by the fact that the names of whistleblowers are stored in the public memory, especially when entire countries become the focus of attention: for example, Julian Assange, Chelsea Manning, or Edward Snowden. Whistleblowers who act against a company as employees are just as spectacular: for example, Jeffrey Wigand, Vice President of Research and Development at the tobacco company Brown & Williamson, brought questionable practices in cigarette production to the public. He passed the information on to Lowell Bergman, a producer of the US news program *60 Minutes*, and to the Food and Drug Administration (FDA) in 1996. According to Wigand, the company had systematically concealed the health risk of the cigarettes it manufactured. This incident was made into a movie worth seeing, *The Insider*, starring Russell Crowe and Al Pacino. Today, Jeffrey Wigand gives lectures, advises public prosecutors, and talks to politicians.

There have also been spectacular incidents in Switzerland: at a media conference in London in January 2011, an employee of a subsidiary of bank Julius Baer, Rudolf Elmer, presented Wikileaks activist Julian Assange with two data carriers that allegedly contained sensitive data records on trusts and offshore structures. He had already posted them on the whistleblower platform in 2007 and 2008, when it was still barely known. In the proceedings against him in Zurich, the prosecution accused him of aiming to destroy the bank's business model and cause maximum damage to the bank's customers. He was also accused of attempting to hand over the data to the then German finance minister,

Peer Steinbrück, on two occasions. The defendant largely denied the allegations, claiming that the data CDs for Assange were empty. And he had not supplied any data to the finance minister either. Elmer was threatened with a prison sentence and a ban from practicing his profession for violating banking secrecy and forgery. On January 19, 2015, he was sentenced to a conditional fine by the District Court of Zurich (Baumgartner 2014, 2015).

Another sensational case was the rotten meat scandal in Germany, uncovered by truck driver Miro Strecker in July 2007. He had loaded frozen cattle eyes, four-year-old mutton livers from New Zealand, and rotting flesh. Such meat may only be used for animal feed at best. To his astonishment, he saw that he was delivering the goods to a producer of meat and sausage products. The goods were to be processed into food. He saw the head of the company unloading the goods alone, which is normally done by the truck drivers. Strecker also observed the boss tearing the labels off the pallets and stuffing them into his trouser pockets. He called the police, but they declared themselves not responsible, as did the Chamber of Industry and Commerce. The trade inspectorate finally listened, and the huge scandal came to light (Prosinger 2013).

As the cases above show, whistleblowing can be classified as an individual or even solitary act of resistance. The individual blows the whistle on what they see as illegal, unethical, or damaging practices by the company to higher authorities within the organization or to bodies outside the organization. The individual can quickly be identified as a renegade and thus easily becomes the target of retaliatory measures by the company. Whistleblowers are usually fired immediately, and if this is not possible, a process is immediately set in motion with the aim of denigrating the whistleblower's performance. However, if it is not possible to prove incompetence, there are cases in which companies have resorted to labeling whistleblowers as crazy or insane (Rothschild and Miethe 1994, p. 253, 264 et seq.).

The full power of the organization is brought to bear on the whistleblowers, who are then left to face the consequences of their actions alone (Edwards et al. 1995, p. 291). Most whistleblowers are not prepared for what happens to them. Few realize beforehand that their excellent performance capabilities over, say, 25 years can turn into a verdict of incompetence overnight.

Whistleblowing raises serious moral and legal questions that lead to contradictory judgments about the act. Whilst whistleblowers like to become heroes in the public eye, they are threatened with years of legal proceedings and often go through extremely stressful phases of their lives before and after the disclosure. Before going public, the question arises as to whether it is worth it, whether you have a chance of being heard, and what personal consequences await you. What should you do if your superior thinks you are allowed to violate environmental regulations, if sexual harassment is constantly swept under the carpet, or if there are massive shortcomings in duty of care?

But also, what to do if you are not 100% sure about the matter and there is nobody who can investigate possible abuses and protect the whistleblower? After disclosure, the organization's far-reaching and drastic retaliatory measures usually take effect immediately. The pressure on the individual is immense. Some lose their job and recognition in their traditional profession, are considered potentially disloyal in the world of work, get into financial difficulties as a result, are confronted with legal proceedings, suffer health problems under the pressure, and often experience family crises, if not tragedies. Some succeed in accepting, organizing, and rebuilding their new reality of life. Others despair and suffer permanently (Rothschild and Miethe 1994, p. 267 et seq.).

A whistleblower is concerned with changing the way work is done in the organization by putting management in their place or forcing them to make changes. Publishing the complaint is the tool to enforce the change that was not possible by other means. This makes whistleblowing a political act. It is triggered by the fact that the existing practices of the organization and the underlying values conflict with those of the whistleblower. This ignites the person's resistance. Management should no longer carry out, support, or accept specific practices, but should be held accountable for them. The management's reaction is also political, in that it attempts to discredit the whistleblower and thus undermine the credibility of their statements. This is the only way to neutralize the validity of the information published by the whistleblower (Rothschild and Miethe 1994, p. 255).

Let us now consider the case of Anne (Rothschild and Miethe 1994, pp. 261–267), a 37-year-old woman who was employed as a foundry mechanic in a company that produced rubber belts. Her job was to mix the chemical substances that made up the rubber. She was happy and grateful to have found the job. After just a few days, she noticed unusual physical reactions, but she continued to work hard. After just two months, her supervisor gave her special praise. She had learned the job faster than anyone else before her. He asked her if she wanted to help him train others. Anne now assumed that she was a valued and valuable employee. A few weeks later, however, she noticed significant physical problems: a burning sensation in her nose and mouth, headaches, and bone pain. At this point, Anne told her supervisor that she wanted to find out more about the chemicals used, their composition, and possible side effects. She noticed that the chemical composition information on individual containers was missing and suggested to the supervisor that he request this information. The supervisor agreed with her and said it was a good idea. The next day she was fired.

After her dismissal, she spoke to other employees and learned that previous workers who had held her position had also been dismissed as soon as they developed health problems. With the help of an industrial hygienist and a toxicologist, she discovered that the company was exposing its workers to chemical substances that were hundreds of times above the level permitted by law. They were also disposing of the toxic waste illegally. As a result of Anne's exposure to the chemicals, she developed a tumor in her mouth and skull and suffered permanent liver damage. The local doctor the company sent her to downplayed the problem. She only found out the full extent of the damage to her health when she consulted independent doctors and experts. Anne set herself the goal of using the media to expose the company's practices to inform the public. Crucial to Anne's politicization was the company's attempt to cover up the abuse and discredit her as critic:

> *"I felt so completely victimized by the company. I had been such a trusting person. When they hired me, I thought they had picked me because they could see that I was an intelligent and responsible person. Now I know that when they picked me, they were picking out a person to murder."*

The paradox in this case was that management was ruthless with the individual and resorted to harsh measures, but it was precisely this retaliation that helped the whistleblower feel vindicated in her moral judgment of how decrepit and corrupt the management was. Once the company had deployed its full arsenal of retaliatory measures, it could no longer go back. Within a short space of time, a battle ensued to discredit the other party decisively.

This and other cases show that whistleblowers are not, as is often assumed, badly disposed and bitter employees, but rather competent and respected individuals from the core workforce who have a strong interest in the organization's reputation. They sincerely believe that disclosing misconduct is in the long-term interests of the company. Crucially, whistleblowers have a strong attachment to principles outside the organization and therefore a lesser attachment to the strict norms of the company. The principles outside the organization are ethical standards that they have acquired, for example, in church, during their professional training, or from their family. And it is precisely this strong adherence to the principles outside the organization that shields them from the pressure within the company, allows them to move on, and gives them the independence they need to do so. Reinforced by the company's retaliation, whistleblowers assume a moral high ground. It is very important for them not to have been involved in the misconduct.

Anne reflected on the events a year and a half after her exposure to the chemical substances and realized that the abuses had been known for over a decade:

> "I ask myself all the time, how can they [her previous bosses] live with themselves? How can they do something like this, knowing they are destroying people's bodies, literally killing them, and causing mutations three generations out? Then I realized that I could never understand them unless I was like them, and I will never be like them."

The special feature of resistance as whistleblowing is therefore that it is not just about questioning practices, beliefs, or authorities. It is also a struggle in which the whistleblower wants to preserve their dignity and integrity.

Before we move on to what an organization can do in relation to whistleblowing, I would like to point out that although the submission of serious complaints qualifies as resistance, it does not always have to be whistleblowing. Complainants do not always bring actual grievances or misconduct to light and rightly denounce them. Whistleblowing must be clearly distinguished from complaints about superiors, which could have been discussed directly with the superior. It can just as well be an attempt to present oneself as a whistleblower, but with a completely different goal: for example, if one tries to make serious accusations against a disliked superior with powerful arguments (e.g. "I don't see any strategy here") or to bully them without being able to prove any substantial wrongdoing. This manifests itself as differences of opinion or even injuries, which are then played out as a hidden game of rivalry. A distinction must therefore be made as to whether the management is being bullied or whether there really is a serious offense that needs to be uncovered. The assessment of such situations must therefore be carried out very carefully and with sufficient time.

Is it just that organizations should take (slightly) less harsh measures in dealing with whistleblowing? This question falls short because the act of resistance to publicly accuse an organization is usually only undertaken if the organization does not address the problem identified by the whistleblower. The organization must embrace the issue of ethics, consider it an important part of its corporate practice and culture, and set out its own stance in its guidelines. However, such guidelines are not enough, as ethical and moral transgressions occur below the visible surface of the organization. Over time, certain unethical practices emerge that can only rarely be traced back to a single individual, such as sexual assault (Ortmann 2011).

Unethical behavior in organizations must therefore be seen as a collective problem. The key to the solution is found in abstract catalogs of values or concrete behavioral guidelines. A code of conduct, core values, compliance guidelines, or similar make it clear that certain values are relevant in the company and that these values are also demanded or can be demanded by members of the organization. However, catalogs of values are often so abstract that individuals do not know how to relate them to their specific work and problem situations.

Behavioral guidelines can only regulate very specific incidents – not other unforeseen ones. Sometimes they are so extensive that people simply do not remember them. If the formal rules and regulations primarily serve to calm people's minds and no one boasts about them in everyday life, they are not effective. The organization and management can therefore not content themselves with demanding compliance from employees. Rather, the members of the organization should be enabled and empowered to be mindful in their everyday work and to make appropriate judgments independently (Ortmann 2011, p. 7 et seq.). However, efforts to promote ethical behavior in organizations must not stop here either, as it must be possible to address the boundaries of what is permissible in everyday life before they are crossed, and even when they have already been crossed. Because then the organization can still solve the problem itself and whistleblowing within the organization does not become whistleblowing outside the organization. However, this is only possible if far-reaching sanctions are not imposed immediately, but if this is seen as an opportunity for the organization to learn and develop. Only then is the individual not left alone with challenging problems, considerations, or even observations of others, but collective responsibility is created in dealing with ethical problems.

## 2.4  Resistance as Organized Industrial Action

By contrast to the previous examples of resistance, this section deals with the organized form of resistance. Industrial action arises from a conflict of interest between employees and employers over the appropriateness of wages and working conditions. Strikes are usually called when previous negotiations have failed, or the strike serves the purpose of emphasizing one's own interests. The resistance is manifested in a strike and documents a clear opposition between the workforce and management. It is then a "hot conflict" (Glasl 2013, p. 76 et seq.) in which the aim is to assert one's own demands. In March 2008, SBB Cargo employees in Bellinzona, Switzerland, went on strike. They finally succeeded in having the redundancy plans withdrawn and a round table set up to work out viable solutions. In Germany, the labor dispute over the 35-hour week made history, but the strike by the German train drivers' union GDL in 2014 and 2015 also caused a stir. In industrial action, however, the strike leaders occasionally also resort to extreme measures. In France, for example, five employees of the Seita tobacco factory went on hunger strike in 2014 to protest the closure of the site in Nantes (Evrard 2014). In 2001, the entire works council of the Opladen railway plant, which was threatened with closure, went on hunger strike to win a long-requested meeting with the minister of economics and transport and the head of the railway company, Mehdorn (Rosenfelder 2003).

Nowadays, trade unions also use newer methods of industrial action to draw attention to their concerns. In 2007, for example, the trade union ver.di called for a flash mob at a Rewe supermarket in Berlin's Ostbahnhof station. People completely paralyzed the supermarket by loading their shopping carts to the brim, only to discover at the checkout that they had left their wallets at home. Or in 2011, 20 supposed guests formed a dance group in a Bremen hotel, singing and drumming and calling for a boycott of the hotel. Prior to this action, the food, beverage, and catering union had failed to win over the employers, and after this action they were able to celebrate a "great wage agreement" (Tornau 2012).

Hunger strikes touch and affect us, public transport strikes annoy some people, while others show understanding. Some of these actions may even make us smile, but we stop laughing when we think of the cashier at the Rewe supermarket. If we take a step back, however, we realize that although we remember individual examples of strikes or other industrial action due to their publicity, strikes are a rather rare phenomenon. On an international comparison of strikes in 20 OECD countries examined, Switzerland, Germany, Japan, and Poland are considered to have particularly low levels of strikes (Lesch 2009). In Western Europe, researchers have concluded that Southern Europe is the "geographical epicenter of current labor disputes." Between 1970 and 1979, the working time lost per thousand employees due to strikes and lockouts amounted to 52 days in Germany and 286 days in France. In the period 2000 to 2007, the number of working days lost was down to 5 in Germany and 103 in France (Vandaele 2014, p. 347).

Despite all the limitations regarding statistical inaccuracies, it can be stated that the number of strike days in Germany and France has gradually declined in recent decades, partly because the frequency and duration of strikes have decreased. Conflicts arising between the social partners are generally settled at the negotiating table. If a strike becomes necessary, its duration and extent are generally very limited (Häubi and Weber 2004, p. 49).

In Austria and Germany, for example, the social partnership (i.e. the cooperative relationship between employers' and employees' associations) has applied since the postwar period. Open conflicts are to be contained and conflicts of interest resolved by consensus. In addition to the traditional political culture, the liberalization of national labor markets has also contributed to this. The growing low-wage sector contributes to declining collective bargaining coverage, but trade unions have also made it possible to make working hours and pay components more flexible in times of crisis to preserve jobs. The liberalization of labor relations at national level can be seen because of the internationalization of economic activity (Behrens 2013).

So much for the findings. But how do those managers who do not directly represent the employer side in the industrial action, but have to keep the business running, perceive the effects of the strike activities? One manager describes his personal management experience during a merger that led to a strike. He reports on two companies that were merged to form a new company. In the first year, there was no new collective labor agreement, but the two existing agreements were continued. According to the manager, the union feared that the new agreement to be negotiated would be worse than the existing, well-paid agreement of one company. The union did everything it could to put pressure on the management of the new company to have favorable arguments for the negotiations. This was at a time when:

*"there were too few staff in many areas and many additional projects were running. A lot of overtime had to be worked. The overload also led to many operational problems, which had a massive impact on employee satisfaction."*

The workforce had many criticisms of the management of the new company. For example, it was criticized that there was a lack of trust in the management. This was demonstrated at an employee information session when the employees left the room in unison during the event. The manager experienced this time as "difficult":

*"Due to the massive shortage, I worked day and night. I tried as best I could to involve the employees in the work. On the other hand, the unions held discussions about the regulation of individual minutes. In this situation, I had no understanding for this. During this time, employees repeatedly gave me personal feedback that they had to behave like this but didn't mean it – in reference to the boycott of the information event. In the meantime, employee satisfaction is very good again. It took years to rebuild trust."*

The resistance organized and orchestrated to better assert specific interests becomes an expression of a relationship of mistrust between employees and top management. The resistance and mistrust are not an expression of the direct management and working relationship, even if the strike, as described here, has a negative impact on cooperation and work performance. In this case, the organized strike maneuvers the employees into an ambivalence between the personal, authentic relationship of trust with their superiors and the organized, staged industrial action. The employees are driven by a guilty conscience because they see and acknowledge the plight of their line manager and presumably many others in the organization. They "don't mean it," so they want to make it clear that their behavior during the strike has nothing to do with the management relationship. They do not want to see their good relationship with their line manager impaired and hope or make sure that their line manager is also understanding toward them.

In the manager's narrative, the employees appear strangely passive, they become followers ("I have to behave like this") of the strike, as they submit to peer pressure and show solidarity with their colleagues and the union. It becomes clear that the employees' solidarity with the union becomes the central instrument of power in the hands of the union, which in turn claims to be fighting for these same employees. The organized strike becomes a potential threat to direct management relations. For this reason, employees reassure themselves of their relationship with their superiors so that the organized power struggle does not permanently damage or destroy the immediate management relationship. Those involved look for a way to overcome the ambivalence between loyalty to the superior and solidarity with the strike movement.

In an organized strike, the employees' institutional relationships with the union and the direct working and management relationships between the employees and their superiors overlap. The insights gained in this section into the complicated structure of relationships made it easier to classify what at first glance may appear to be irritating behavior and not, for example, to understand it a priori as an expression of a deteriorating management relationship.

## Summary

- Overt resistance is usually clearly visible, audible, and is usually quickly recognized and designated as resistance.

- If resistance appears to be an emphatically expressed demand, either a process is initiated in which it is seriously addressed or the demand is rejected as unreasonable. Resistance is likely to be successful if employees or managers persistently defend their demands.

- Resistance can be experienced as part of an open and seemingly endless power struggle that is very difficult to overcome.

- Resistance is also expressed when a person speaks out against certain practices of the organization and thus against the entire company. In this case, we speak of whistleblowing.

- Organized industrial action is often the first thing associated with resistance in organizations, but it happens very rarely. In industrial action, institutional relations between the workforce and the unions overlap with management relations. If one is not aware of this, those relations may deteriorate.

# CHAPTER

# 3

# Covert Resistance

Everyday forms of resistance make no headlines. Just as millions of anthozoan polyps create, willy-nilly, a coral reef, so do thousands upon thousands of individual acts of insubordination and evasion create a political or economic barrier reef on their own.

—James C. Scott

In the previous chapter, we talked about resistance that tends to be loud, explicit, and confrontational. This chapter is about resistance that is covert or quiet. This subtle form of resistance often takes place anonymously and the resistors are thus lulled into a sense of security. This form of resistance can be inconspicuous and unnoticed at first, and sometimes even charming, but it also influences organizations and management and leadership relationships.

As Scott (1985, 1986) and Fleming and Sewell (2002) suggest, the unfinished novel *The Adventures of the Good Soldier Schwejk* by

Jaroslav Hašek (2013) serves as an example of more inconspicuous resistance. The novel is set in Prague at the time of the imperial-royal Austro-Hungarian monarchy at the beginning of the twentieth century. Josef Schwejk resigned from military service years ago after he was "finally declared stupid by the military medical commission." The anti-hero of the little people makes ends meet by selling dogs with fake pedigrees. The First World War breaks out and the Austrian authorities call up Schwejk. At the garrison hospital, he comes to the attention of the field curate Katz who takes him on as a servant. Whilst playing cards, the field curate gambles Schwejk away to First Lieutenant Lukasch. Schwejk assists the lieutenant as an officer's servant during his amorous escapades. The good times end abruptly when Schwejk gives the lieutenant-colonel a stolen dog and Lukasch then meets Colonel Kraus, who turns out to be the dog's previous owner. The colonel orders Lieutenant-Colonel Lukasch and Schwejk with him to the 91st Infantry Regiment in Budweis. On the train journey from Prague to Budweis, Schwejk pulls the emergency brake, leaves the train, drinks the fare, and has to walk to Budweis. On this march, he is mistaken for a spy and is supposed to be executed in the Przemyśl fortress but is saved by chance and sent back to his regiment in Budweis. When the 91st Regiment is transferred to Bruck an der Leitha, he mistakenly delivers a love letter from Lieutenant Lukasch to the husband of his beloved, which leads to a wild brawl, and Schwejk destroys the love letter by eating it. Another train journey by the 91st Regiment is chaotic and inefficient. Finally, Schwejk marches toward the front and encounters an escaped Russian prisoner of war bathing in a pond. Out of curiosity, he puts on the Russian uniform and becomes an Austrian prisoner of war. After some effort, Schwejk succeeds in convincing his guards that he is not Russian. General Fink wants to have him executed as a spy without further ado but has the 91st Regiment make enquiries. The pious and bland field curate Martinec tries to offer Schwejk spiritual consolation before the execution but fails completely because Schwejk tells him stories all the time and doesn't let him get a word in edgewise. Much to the general's displeasure, a telegram arrives telling him that Schwejk is to be sent back to his company immediately.

Over the course of more than 500 pages, Schwejk experiences hair-raising adventures and drives many of those he encounters to despair. It is worth taking a closer look at very specific episodes to better grasp the subtle background to the novel. To this end, a scene from director Wolfgang Lieben's 13-part television series produced by ORF and ZDF in 1972, which takes place at the beginning of the novel, is reproduced below. Schwejk is arrested for defamation and treason, released, and arrested again. The following dialog is on the original soundtrack. In the series, Schwejk speaks in Austrian-Czech gibberish:

| | |
|---|---|
| *Police officer:* | "I'm very sorry that you've fallen into our hands again. We hoped that you might mend your ways. But we were wrong." |
| *Schwejk:* | "Dear sir, unfortunately appearances are sometimes deceptive." |
| *Police officer:* | "Don't behave so stupidly. It is certainly very unpleasant for us to keep you in custody, and I can assure you that in my opinion your guilt is not that great. With your low intelligence, you have undoubtedly been misled. [Then quieter and slower] Tell me, Mr. Schwejk, who induces you to do such stupid things?" |
| *Schwejk* [coughs]: | "Dear sir, I know of no stupidity." |
| *Police officer:* | "Well, isn't it stupid of you to cause a crowd in front of the war |

|                               |                                                                                                                                                                                                                                                                                                    |
|-------------------------------|----------------------------------------------------------------------------------------------------------------------------------------------------------------------------------------------------------------------------------------------------------------------------------------------------|
|                               | manifesto and stir up the people by shouting? Hail Emperor Franz Josef! We will win this war!" [sighs]                                                                                                                                                                                              |
| *Schwejk:*                    | "Dear sir, forgive me. But I couldn't stay idle. I was so excited. I've seen how people stand in front of the war manifesto and how they read it, and there's no joy, no cheers, no hurrahs, no nothing. As if … as if this is none of people's business. You can't remain inactive." *Police officer* [nods]. |
| *Schwejk:*                    | "Look, if there's already a war, then you have to win it, then you have to shout the emperor up. Nobody will talk me out of it. Or … would you have … shouted down?"                                                                                                                                 |
| *Police officer* [grumbling]: | "Go to the devil. You're discharged. [And then louder] But if you come here again, I won't question you anymore and you'll go straight to the military court on Hradschin. Do you understand?"                                                                                                       |
| *Schwejk:*                    | "Yes, yes. [Shakes the Chief of Police's hand with thanks and kisses it] Thank you sir a thousand times. (…) And sir, please, if you ever need a dog. Just turn to me with confidence, dear sir. Because I have a dog business."                                                                     |

The *police officer* [rolls his eyes, holds his forehead and turns away in despair].

Schwejk is simply declared by the police officer to be not entirely sane. It is therefore impossible for him to have carried out the agitation on his own initiative, and therefore he cannot be prosecuted. Schwejk behaves submissively and subserviently and insists on his unreserved loyalty to state authority. His behavior is obviously inflammatory, but his declared intention is to strengthen public order. The fact that he also wants to sell the police officer a dog at the end shows that he doesn't seem to recognize the seriousness of his situation, which in turn underlines his alleged stupidity. The police officer is exasperated and finally glad to be rid of Schwejk, who saved himself and saves himself many more times in the novel.

Schwejk takes orders literally, fulfills his duty excessively, and overfulfills his obedience to orders. At the same time, he displays behavior that can be interpreted as sabotage, for example, by constantly talking down to others, preferably those in authority, and not letting them have their say. The "Schwejk attitude" is named after him, a destructive "letting things go to waste" (Bömelburg 2011, p. 192). Schwejk drives some people mad, or at least almost. Whilst others are sentenced to years in prison, he just manages to escape and obtains minor advantages and comforts for himself. Schwejk is certainly no revolutionary, but with his comedy, his flaunted naivety, and his peasant shrewdness, he manages to stay happily within the system and not let things get too bad for him. Nevertheless, he just as shamelessly exposes the nonsense of the system and the hierarchy and reduces it to absurdity with his behavior.

Schwejk "is not a character designed to develop; we learn almost nothing about him, his parents, or his origins" (Bömelburg

2011, p. 186). Is he really as stupid as he seems, or is he cunning? Is he playing with authority and showing it off or does he simply recognize it? Does he have a grand plan or is it just luck? Is he brave, bold, and clever or just naive? Why does he always get by? The answer to these questions is quite simple: we don't know. Obviously, he goes through life with his humor and curiosity in a carefree and cheerful manner, but this also gets him into seemingly hopeless situations time and again. However, he maneuvers his way out of the mess and then goes on his way again unscathed. What is relevant here is that his behavior is perceived by superiors as naïve, stupid, pushy, but also charming and entertaining. He is never at a loss for an answer that unquestionably proves his obedience.

Schwejk is not an agitator or revolutionary and therefore poses no serious threat to the authorities. They even feel somewhat flattered by him and for the most part do not notice how the nonsense and absurdities of the system are revealed in conversation with Schwejk. In the novel, Schwejk stands for an elusive criticism of the system. This criticism is hidden, and the actual motives cannot really be fathomed. Because the criticism does not explicitly question the authorities or is charmingly disguised with humor, obedience, and irony, the authorities do not experience themselves as being attacked. Nevertheless, the resistance is latently perceptible: intentional or innocent, entertaining or annoying, inciting or system-stabilizing. Resistance here cannot be analyzed down to the last detail and is not at all unambiguous.

The researcher Contu (2008) calls this form of resistance "decaffeinated." You could also say it is a toothless tiger. But we can't make it that easy for ourselves. It would be too easy to overvalue the real resisters and agitators and devalue the hidden resisters. As we will see, hidden resistance also affects the relationship between management and employees, even if some managers report that at some point they no longer hear about the resistance or dismiss it as gossip. They then conclude that the resistance no longer exists or that broad acceptance has now been achieved. In doing so, they may just be closing their eyes and overlooking something essential. The absence of open resistance or dissenting statements does not indicate approval and satisfaction or even an insight into the meaningfulness of changes or management decisions (Fleming and Spicer 2008, p. 303). As we will see, it may well be that quiet resistance points to important disruptions, deficits, or blockages. This form of resistance is therefore of fundamental importance for the strength and developmental capacity of organizations but also for the well-being of organizations.

## 3.1 Resistance as Humor

*Question on Radio Yerevan:* "Can you eat the mushrooms from Chernobyl again?"

*Radio Yerevan:* "In principle yes, but you must not have your toilet connected to the public sewage system."

Organizations are far from perfect. However, management concepts or even the language of management like to suggest a smooth and coherent organizational world. This contradiction alone invites some kind of confrontation. Humor is a response, a reaction to this, and, according to the Duden dictionary, is to be understood as a person's gift to face the inadequacy of the world and its people and the difficulties and misfortunes of everyday life with cheerful composure. Humor means not despairing at the unfortunate events of the world. It brings something to light and reveals or makes visible what people experience as absurd or contradictory in everyday life. Humor can be understood as a gift or as a human attitude. A humorous comment always conveys a certain message or concern. Humor makes it possible to protect the person who uses humor from the consequences of the statements made. There is something playful and unreal about humorous statements, and they protect the speaker from serious consequences. People can express problematic content with less fear of being rejected or attacked or of being exposed to counter accusations (Grugulis 2002; p. 388).

A joke and laughing at a joke are a crucial aspect of humor. There are jokes that are simply funny and universal. An example: Two hunters are walking through the forest. Suddenly one of them collapses. The other calls the ambulance: "My friend is dead. What should I do?" The emergency doctor: "First make sure he's really dead." Then a shot rings out. "Okay," says the hunter to the emergency doctor, "now what?" However, a joke is not necessarily perceived as funny, either because the joke itself is considered indecent or because it makes use of worn-out clichés. When members of organizations make jokes, they can also be directed at people or processes within the organization. Either everyone laughs at a funny comment and has a shared sense of what is humorous. Or some people laugh, and others don't feel like laughing at all because they feel attacked, ridiculed, or pilloried. But only in rare cases does an ill-timed joke become dangerous for the joke teller, as shown in a short scene in the German feature film *Das Leben der Anderen (The Lives of Others)* from 2006. The film takes a critical look at the history of the GDR by portraying the workings of state security. In one scene in a Stasi canteen, the protagonist, Stasi captain Gerd Wiesler, has lunch with his superior, called Grubitz. The Stasi sub-lieutenant Axel Stigler sits down at a nearby table with his work colleagues and is about to tell a Honecker joke. He starts to tell his joke, but then realizes that his colleagues are silent and embarrassed. Only now does Stigler realize that Grubitz is there. He tries to apologize, to talk his way out of it. Grubitz asks him to continue the joke. He probably already knew the joke anyway. Stigler then recounts: "Honecker … the General Secretary … sees the sun and says: "Good morning, dear sun." The sun replies: "Good morning, dear Erich." And at midday, Erich goes to the window again, opens it, sees the sun and says: "Good day, dear sun." And the sun says: "Good day, dear Erich." And after work, Honecker goes to the window again and says: "Good evening, dear sun." And the sun says nothing. So, he asks again: "Good evening, dear sun. What's wrong?" And then the sun says: "Kiss my ass, Honecker, I'm in the West now!" Grubitz laughs heartily and looks at the sub-lieutenant. He asks abruptly and with a serious expression: "Name, rank, department? (…) I don't need to tell you what this means for your career, what you've just done. (…) What you did was mock the party. That was incitement and certainly only the tip of the iceberg. I will report this to the minister's office." The sub-lieutenant slumps down, completely stunned. Suddenly Grubitz laughs and says: "I was only joking" and adds another joke. "What's the difference between a telephone and Honecker? None at all! Hang up, dial again." At the end of the film, the viewer realizes that Stigler has been demoted.

The Stasi sub-lieutenant Axel Stigler simply tells the "good joke" at the wrong time and in the presence of the wrong person. The example shows that jokes can indeed have very negative consequences. Stigler wants to make fun of state authorities amongst his work colleagues, a common practice at the time. These jokes were probably also made by the representatives of state authorities amongst themselves, but not in the presence of the common people. The sub-lieutenant overlooks the fact that a representative of the state authorities is present and underestimates the danger this poses for him. He understands he is only allowed to repeat such jokes amongst his peers, but because of

Grubitz's request, he is under the misapprehension that this rule will be suspended for a moment.

In this context, it is not about humor per se or a humorous person, but about the use of humor as an expression of resistance in organizations. Let's start with an example from a whole host of managers' own experiences. A sales manager and member of the management board of a company in the electronics and computer technology sector was looking for ways to increase efficiency in sales through new tools and processes. The sales manager expected significant efficiency gains, as many processes had grown generically over the years. From the management's point of view, the existing, unsystematic data storage server was inefficient. The folder structures had grown over the years. From the management's perspective, selective access rights led to a pronounced "bunker mentality" and to people cultivating their own little gardens. Documents were filed multiple times and documents that were thought to be lost had to be searched for over a long period. To solve the problem with a "root canal treatment," the management decided to introduce a filing system, called A-P-DOK, in the company. Resistance was "preprogrammed," as the management interfered with the individual working methods of all employees. The manager describes that the resistance was multifaceted. He particularly remembers the repeated jokes:

> *"I can't find my clothes in the morning because I've sorted them by A-P-DOK at home."*

The management's intended effect of ensuring order with the new filing system is made ridiculous in this case: the system is not even able to solve a trivial task (organizing clothes), so how is it supposed to solve the far more complex operational task? At first glance, this ironic turn of phrase raises doubts about the promised effectiveness of the newly introduced system.

In a subtle way, employees make their criticism and skepticism transparent. They consider the system to be inadequate and make fun of it, but also of the management responsible for introducing the system. However, this humorous comment is probably not just a criticism of the fact that the new system is not considered to be efficient. The employees obviously do not identify with the solution; the joke expresses their disassociation. This is because the management made the decision without involving the employees, which clearly places the responsibility for the (alleged) dysfunctionality of the solution on those responsible for the implementation (i.e. the management). However, there is likely to be another problem. Based on the manager's account, it can be assumed that there was an unannounced intervention in a work organization that is perceived as personal or private, which is then perceived as a severe loss of autonomy. Finally, the old work organization is also judged to be inefficient, with efficiency gains being attributed to the new system. Behind what at first glance appears to be an odd management initiative, this brief example already allows us to make some assumptions as to the reasons for the resistance. But conclusions can also be drawn for forward-looking management action: the example shows that employees behave in a resistant manner when they are unable to participate in a solution that also has a negative impact on their autonomy at work and when the previous way of working is devalued, albeit implicitly.

Let's move on to another example that is not about operational optimization, but about a moral programming attempt. Westwood and Johnston (2012) examined the Australian lottery company Lucky Treasure. Among the 350 employees, the ratio of men to women was roughly balanced, with men holding most of the management positions. The company implemented a program designed to promote gender equality in the workplace, although the lottery company described itself as having an open and collaborative culture and claimed very low levels of harassment and discrimination. Nevertheless, it was felt that such a program was necessary. The organization apparently assumed that it was possible for all employees to have the same understanding of harassment, that a shared understanding of appropriate and respectful behavior could be communicated to employees, and that employees would comply. The human resources (HR) department ensured that people of different genders were represented in the various workshops and that the groups were made up of people from different departments and hierarchical levels. The aim was to bring together people who did not know each other from the immediate work context to counteract anonymity within the company. This anonymity was identified as a breeding ground for inappropriate behavior. Nevertheless, it was not entirely possible to avoid people knowing each other and sitting next to each other in the workshops.

A similar program had been implemented once before. However, the workshops back then were considered overly legalistic by employees, and an external consultant concluded that it would not have suited the company's benevolent, spirited, and socially minded culture. The workshops needed to be more fun and interactive. The HR managers used fun material that also had a work context. They decided to show film clips from the well-known comedy TV series *The Office*. This TV series was adapted for German-language television under the title *Stromberg*.

In the original television series, a documentary team follows the everyday office life of the fictitious company, which is called Capitol Versicherung AG in the German-language version. The action mostly takes place in the claims settlement department M-Z. Women, gay and lesbian workers, immigrants, weaker employees, the disabled, and socially marginalized groups are mocked, exposed, or humiliated throughout. The protagonist of the series is department head Bernd Stromberg, who knows how to exploit this game to his own advantage. He sees himself as infallible, admitting at most that there are superiors who are better at their job. In this respect, he is probably the blatant antithesis of social competence: he behaves opportunistically, avoids direct confrontation, abuses others for his own career goals, etc. To put it simply, Stromberg is the tip of this iceberg.

These shows are a parody of the world of modern management and the political correctness demanded by society and companies. Most people would interpret Stromberg's behavior as completely inappropriate, insulting, and degrading. Stromberg shows behavior that breaks with all the expectations placed on employees and managers in today's organizations. This was precisely the interpretation that the HR managers expected from the workshop participants.

Short scenes were shown in the workshop with the intention of loosening up the topic a little and then working out the serious issues together with the workshop participants. It turned out quite differently. Excerpts were commented on with smiles, laughter, and comments, such as the following:

*"Just like my last workplace!"*
*"Oh, he's a problem child, isn't he?"*
*"What a jerk!"*

The workshop participants grinned and chuckled maliciously at almost every variation of politically incorrect behavior. After the excerpts, the facilitators divided the participants into groups and asked them to complete a short questionnaire to identify different forms of discrimination and harassment. Participants were then asked to name the identified behaviors and the facilitators wrote them down on the white board. General merriment ensued and the discussion eventually led to the question of what constitutes sexual harassment. However, the employees came up with completely different interpretations than those provided by the HR department and joked about it. For example, one participant, Jack, mused about a comment on a woman's legs in a movie clip from the TV series. Sitting right next to Jack was Jenny, who worked in the same department as him. They both seemed to get on well and like each other:

> *Jack: "But I comment on Jenny's legs every day!"*
> *Jenny laughs out loudly, as does the rest of the room.*
> *Another employee chips in asking: "What if 'Lisa with the long legs' doesn't find that offensive? What if she's flattered?"*
> *Another female employee adds: "Yes, that's a compliment!"*

The HR manager does not know what is happening to him and reacts quickly by asking:

> *"How does the manager know she is flattered? What if she wasn't? (…) It really is inappropriate to make a comment on a person's appearance like that, not something as personal."*

Jenny reacts immediately and jokes:

> *"Oh jeez, I've been commenting on Jack's butt for ages, to which Jack pretends he's deeply offended."*

Again, everyone in the room laughs and the HR manager tries to return to a more serious tone by focusing on the legalistic argument:

> *"It's really pretty risky to make personal, appearance-related comments that could be interpreted as suggestive or 'lewd.'"*

The attempt to correct the jokes and behavior of the employees was questioned and undermined by the employees throughout the workshop. With examples of harassment in posters, caricatures, e-mails, screensavers, or casual remarks, the participants took the mickey out of each other. The moderator was repeatedly challenged, and his answers were not convincing. But even after the workshop, employees continued to make fun of him. One employee asked another to lend him a pen, to which the latter replied in an exaggeratedly whiny voice:

*"You're just harassing me now."*

Before I reflect on the case, I would like to make it clear that I am not trying to trivialize or relativize sexual harassment. I also believe that organizations should tackle the problem, because the effects cause damage to the victims, and to the organization.

The situation in which everyone finds themselves is humorous. An HR department wants to convey serious messages to the employees with humor, and the employees undermine this intention with humor. The situation also contains a certain irony, as the HR department clearly wants to encourage employees to be careful with humor but does not use humor very carefully in the preparation and design of the workshop itself. It does not reflect on the fact that there could also be other reactions than the one it has planned. The HR department even causes the problematic behavior in the first place through the workshop design, or it brings behavior to the surface that it assumed did not exist.

But what does this have to do with resistance? The organization obviously wants to hear certain interpretations from its employees. It wants to avoid possible legal disputes and a loss of image for the company. The employees are not fundamentally opposed to this intention, but to the organization's request to equip them with very specific moral principles. They simply do not want to be and think exactly as the organization would like them to. The organization does not want to entertain with a humorous opening; it instrumentalized humor to better anchor its legitimate legalistic concerns in people's minds. The employees perceive the organization as insincere and inauthentic, especially regarding the true, legalistic motives of the program. What comes across as humorous is meant in all seriousness.

Employees should think and then do what the organization deems appropriate. During implementation, however, the organization realizes that the intended humor produces unintended humor, which is then directed against the organization's intention. Put simply, it backfires. It fails in raising awareness of sexual harassment; instead, a masculine culture is made (newly) acceptable. However, it is not just men who take part in this game, but also women, who are just as active. This suggests that the employees are only superficially rejecting management's interpretations of sexual harassment but are trying to resist the attempt by management to control and direct their thoughts and feelings.

Humor can therefore serve to challenge the authority of management and the status quo. The humor shown here is resistant and subversive, but not entirely seditious. Radcliffe-Brown (1952) describes this quality of humor as a "permissible irreverence" that subtly suggests a difference of opinion. With this type of humor, the individual can simply let off steam without seeking to undermine or destroy the status quo or be punished for doing so (Grugulis 2002).

What conclusions can be drawn here for management? In this specific case, the management packaged its messages rather clumsily, thus losing credibility and no longer being taken seriously. During the conception phase, management could have realized that it was setting itself a trap from which there would be no escape during the workshop. The HR department was concerned with identifying certain inappropriate behavior and asking the participants to refrain from it. Instead of trying to prevent certain behavior, the training could have reflected on existing practice and, if necessary, problematized it and explored alternative forms of behavior together with the participants.

## 3.2 Resistance as Cynical Distancing

*A scenario I personally saw acted out ... by several different workers involved a foreman stopping to talk to a worker in a non-work-related, seemingly friendly conversation. The worker would be smiling and conversing congenially, yet the moment the foreman turned to walk away, the worker would make an obscene gesture (usually involving the middle finger) behind the foreman's back, so that all other workers could clearly see.*

From: Beef processing plant (Thompson 1983, p. 222)
( found in Ashforth and Mael 1998)

Let's imagine the following situation: a project team comes together for a meeting. Individual project team members are extremely dissatisfied with the start and progress of the project. They originally did not want to participate in the project but were forced out of their position. They feel that they have hardly any room to maneuver in the project and that they are being overloaded with additional work. The project manager starts the presentation, and a picture of a black cat appears at the top right of the slide – obviously copied from the PowerPoint symbol menu. The project manager has tried to find a suitable symbolic image. The title of the project reads like the name of a predator. As soon as the symbol appears, one of the meeting participants shouts out loud: "That's not a predator, it's a neutered tomcat." Everyone at the meeting laughs, the project manager stands there like a poodle, tries to keep his composure, and starts the presentation. Is that humorous, ironic, sarcastic, or cynical? It all depends. Some meeting participants may simply find it funny; others appreciate the irony; others love the mockery and agree. The project manager didn't find it funny and probably felt mocked and humiliated.

As we saw in the previous section, one of the purposes of humor is to distance oneself from specific projects of an organization or from the organization as a whole. Successful humor is funny, but not always funny for those at whom the humor is aimed. Another type of distancing is (perceived) cynicism. A cynical comment usually no longer elicits laughter. It expresses the fact that the speaker has an opposing view. A possible injury to the other person does not stop the speaker from making the comment.

Excessively frequent cynical comments during or about work can be interpreted as a sign of approaching exhaustion. An art director who suffered a burnout remembers the time before the event. Others told her back then that she complained a lot. But she didn't perceive herself that way. Over time, she realized that she was always reacting cynically to job assignments, such as: "Yes, of course, then I can also design the birthday card for the grandmother of the customer's friend" (Wagner 2011).

However, cynicism can also be a form of expression for organizational resistance. Let's take the following situation as an example: an employee of the fast-food chain McDonald's was sent to an in-house training program in which she and her colleagues were trained in quality, teamwork, cleanliness, and much more. The employee completed the training flawlessly. But she was extremely cynical about her company and, in her opinion, saw through management's real motives. She expressed this cynicism by secretly wearing a "McShit" T-shirt under her work clothes. She worked efficiently, like every team member, and seemed outwardly committed to the company, but her attitude betrayed something else. She acted as if she believed and lived the prescribed values of the organization. Does this harm the organization? As described, probably not. The rejection of the company's mission and the non-identification with the company do not become a problem for the company (Fleming and Spicer 2003, p. 166). The superficial staging of identification is sufficient for the company because the workforce is just as efficient as everyone else and like those workers who identify strongly with the company.

A similar observation can be made in a study of the American high-tech company Tech (Kunda 1992, pp. 26–109). At the time of the study, Tech was an internationally recognized company, was extremely profitable, and controlled a substantial part of the market. Tech's products were at the cutting edge of technology. Top management believed that Tech was a very special company and communicated this systematically in documents and codified principles, speeches, and interviews. Certain values were repeated and communicated repeatedly, if not relentlessly, in various contexts: honesty, responsibility, people orientation, justice, fairness, profit, performance orientation, enthusiasm, personal development. In terms of official company language, however, some employees agreed in private that "a load of bullshit" was heard in groups and meetings.

At Tech, employees often met in person, for example, during speeches, presentations, meetings, lectures, celebrations, or workshops. During presentations, managers talked about technical and business matters, but also used them to address key values. This was also the case at the presentation entitled "Tech's Strategy for the 90s" by Dave Carpenter, a long-serving manager at the company. The Lyndsville site had only recently been transferred to his area of responsibility. The presentation was his first at this location and was considered a special event. All employees at the property were invited. The presentation took place in the company's largest conference room, called "Einstein." Most of the managers, many engineers, and several staff members were present. By 2:30 p.m., all the seats were taken, even though the presentation didn't start until 3 p.m. By the time the presentation began, the conference room was completely full. The room's décor underscored the importance of the occasion: the lectern was located below an etching of the room's namesake, a large screen hung above the stage, the presentation equipment was state-of-the-art, and a camera recorded the event. Three minutes before 3 p.m., Dave Carpenter took to the stage with Jack, a manager reporting directly to him. Jack announced Dave with the words:

> *"We finally have Dave here. Our seminar series often features outside speakers, but it is hard to get top management here. So, block him as he heads for the door."*

Some smiled, some laughed. Jack waited a few seconds and then added in a slightly more solemn tone:

> *"Like many of us in Engineering, Dave came up the hard way through the ranks. He knows what it takes to get them up and out the door. He is one of us."*

Dave seemed to agree with what was said, adjusted the microphone, nodded imperceptibly to the video camera, and began to speak:

> *"It's a pleasure being here. It justifies the work we do and gives meaning to being in Tech. The further you get away from people, the more you miss the past! You are doing a good and important job. I know you're having fun; and you're doing good work, really neat things. You're the perfect example of what we mean by "bottom-up." (...) Now let me tell you about the challenges we are facing and the role of your group in what lies ahead."*

He added:

> *"I gave this presentation yesterday at the Jackson group; I pulled the slides out from my road show. I hope they're in the right order."*

The sharing of backstage information and the self-irony are to be understood as signals to the audience that he feels completely at home among the technicians and belongs to them. The lights went out. The room went dark, and the first very professionally designed slide appeared on the big screen behind Dave. An audience member, a true veteran of such events, whispered:

*"Here we go, we're on air."*

This was followed by remarks about the "We Are One" strategy, in which Dave said, for example:

*"The challenges are great, but we're well ahead of the competition, we can kill them in the marketplace. There are three main pieces to the strategy. First, we want to be the quality vendor and the vendor of choice. Not only be but be perceived to be [smile] by the customer."*

Dave explained the strategy further and went into great technical detail. The silent crowd seemed to be carried away by the speaker's enthusiasm. The audience acknowledged his snide remarks about the competition with laughter, nodded in agreement, and some took notes. A sense of togetherness was palpable in this pleasant, almost intimate, semi-dark presentation. This was emphasized, evoked, and expressed by Dave's constant use of the word "we."

But not everyone was one heart and one soul. Some employees left the room during the presentation; for the administrative staff the presentation seemed like a "party for the high earners," and for individual engineers and managers it was a "waste of time" at best. An engineer commented during the presentation:

*"I don't need all that happy horseshit. (...) It's the old song and dance, and you hear about it anyway."*

After the presentation, participants were able to ask questions. Dave sat down and took questions like the following:

*"Dave, given what you've said about finance, from where we are sitting, what single thing could we do to help you fulfill your needs?"*

An engineer, obviously annoyed by the overenthusiastic tone, commented on the question, clearly audible to the people around him:

*"Gimme a break."*

The events at Tech all followed a very similar pattern. Critical points were also openly addressed at a corresponding meeting over lunch. Afterwards, the participants came together informally and looked back on the event. Some were enthusiastic, others cynical:

*"These speeches are just endless, like in the Kremlin."*

On such occasions, managers emphasize the community and strive to arouse collective interest. The audience behaves passively, is addressed in an undifferentiated way, and is expected to confirm what is being said. Some fulfill these expectations, others do not. The latter engage in role distancing (Goffman 1961, p. 108): they mock the pompous official rituals of management or the submissive and, in their view, ingratiating comments of colleagues. They distance themselves from the event with cynical comments to reveal hidden meanings, parody customs, and make it clear that they are aware of the theatrical nature of the event. These employees claim to have recognized or exposed the real, hypocritical, or even exploitative practices of the management and maintain a cynical distance from them. And yet, these employees of the organization also provide their services. This means that they behave in everyday organizational and management life as if they did not have this knowledge or attitude at all. Cynicism, it can be concluded, gives us the feeling that we cannot be completely reduced to the corporate role, but that we are unique individuals (Fleming and Spicer 2003, p. 164) who cannot be completely absorbed by the organization. Cynical comments heard directly or indirectly can come across as a slap in the face to those to whom they are directed or who relate them to themselves, as ungrateful mockery, or as a devaluation of honest, if not self-sacrificing, efforts on behalf of the organization. It may not be easy not to be taken in by this insulting effect, but it probably helps to be aware that cynical distancing helps you to experience yourself as an independent person.

## 3.3 Resistance Between Submissive Overfulfillment and Subtle Refusal

In the previous section, we learned about the behavior of employees who ostensibly agree with the management, but then cynically criticize the management alone or amongst themselves. The surface is polished clean so that the person cannot be blamed for anything. This section is mainly about exploring different approaches that serve to keep up appearances – just like Schwejk, who could never really be proven guilty of anything. Supervisors cannot confront employees with offenses because there is simply nothing to accuse them of. Employees do what is expected of them and cannot be convicted of any wrongdoing.

We are all familiar with the description of those types of people who make themselves submissive allies of management and organizational norms to gain a concrete advantage, usually a promotion. There are plenty of disparaging terms for this, and they need not be repeated here. The phenomenon of overachievement is not meant here, but rather behaviors that are characterized by exaggerated approval, but which are not linked to the expectation of wanting to climb the career ladder. Exaggerated and flaunted enthusiasm or compliance with the prevailing norms can be an expression of the opposite, namely skepticism or rejection, without this skepticism or rejection being directly visible or addressable. The members of the organization, like our good soldier Schwejk, want to get by, not offend, and feel they are on safe ground. Nothing should be held against them.

However, employees of an organization can also refer to very specific principles enshrined in the organization's guiding principles, such as empowerment, equality, or participation, and insist that these must now actually be implemented. In doing so, they demand the fulfillment of this one standard. Employees can also become advocates of a single principle, such as customer orientation, and put the interests of the customer before the interests of the company. For example, a salesperson may sell a customer a cheaper product even though the customer could and would afford a more expensive one. Or he can refrain from selling a customer additional service, even though he knows very well that he could succeed in doing so if only he would (Fleming and Spicer 2003, p. 172 et seq.).

Another expression is "service by the book," the inflexible adherence to what you are directly employed for and what you are explicitly instructed to do. Anything that goes beyond this is no longer done: information is not passed on, additional work is not taken on, the colleague or supervisor is not made aware of upcoming problems, you don't stand in for a sick colleague, or the customer is not helped if this is not explicitly intended. As a result, procedures are delayed, new problems creep in, and the behavior is met with incomprehension. But what is there to criticize? The person fulfills exactly the task for which they are employed. An example of this is the go-slow strike by German air traffic controllers in 1973, when they did not leave the workplace but significantly reduced their actual work performance.

In the case of work to rule, the work is still performed on the surface, but there are decisive omissions at work. On the other hand, shirking and time-wasting can also be an expression of resistance. For example, the American tap manufacturer Water Saver reported that employees spent an excessive amount of time in the toilet and 19 employees had to justify themselves for excessive toilet use. Cell phones were banned in the factory and the company manager suspected that his employees were spending time in the restroom making phone calls and texting. The factory tried to prevent this shirking by only allowing access to the toilets with a personal access card. This also made it possible to record the time. People were not allowed to stay in the toilet for longer than six minutes. The company boss Steve Kersten told the US television station CNN that they had no other choice and that 120 production hours were lost in May 2014 alone because workers had wasted so much time in the toilets. Is this a case of resistance? Without more detailed knowledge of the situation, it is difficult to say for sure. One hypothesis could be that the employees disregarded internal company regulations because they had the impression that they were being excessively restricted and patronized, as the company was constantly imposing more rigid regulations and becoming increasingly petty.

The list of imaginative dawdling is very long: pretending to be busy, for example, by constantly holding the phone to your ear without actually making a call. Running across the corridor with work documents and rushing into colleagues' offices, but only chatting to your colleagues there. Completing work for the boss quickly but lagging on work for colleagues. Doing all the work that is personally assigned to you very quickly, but leaving the work that is in the general pool. If this is deliberately and systematically intended to reduce the company's performance by impairing the workflow, it can also be described as sabotage.

An extremely revealing study by Jim Scott from 1986 (pp. 9–17) provides insights into this practice and, above all, into the background and motives of the resisters. Scott dealt with very concrete, everyday resistance by farmers in Malaysia. The study shows how subtly resistance can be articulated in hidden refusal to work and provides insights for resistance in organizations. Scott reports from 1975 on a Malaysian village in a rice-growing region. A group of women who planted and harvested rice plants by hand tried to boycott landowners who wanted to borrow combine harvesters with the aim of reducing the amount of manual labor. The women typically also harvested the fields where they had previously planted rice. With the use of machines, they would have lost about half of their seasonal income. Understandably, they took offense at planting rice for those landowners who used machines for harvesting. They began to organize a quiet but collective boycott by refusing to plant rice for these landowners. Three out of five women's groups attempted the boycott, with the two non-boycotting groups refusing to break the boycott. They also did not work for the boycotted landowners. The three groups did not engage in direct confrontation but spread rumors and made insinuations. They let it be known through intermediaries that the group was not happy about the loss of harvesting labor and was reluctant to plant rice in the fields where the machines had been used in the previous season. They also said that if a machine broke down during the harvest, the landowner could not count on them to bail him out. When the irrigation season arrived and it was time to make good on the threat, caution prevailed. They did not boycott the relevant landowners but stalled. They told them that they were busy elsewhere and could not come to their fields yet. Only a dozen farmers had used harvesters in the previous season, so the women actually had a lot of other work to do, and the reasoning was plausible. The farmers were concerned and became increasingly worried as the best time for planting was slowly slipping away. After more than two weeks of standoff, 6 of the 12 landowners indirectly indicated that they were planning to hire laborers outside the village to plant their rice. The boycott quickly collapsed as more and more women refused to continue. They hastily passed on the news that they would start work in the next few days. Three landowners changed their minds and hired the women, but three landowners hired workers outside the village because they thought it was too late to cancel. Or they wanted to teach the women a lesson.

In today's working world, there are similar indirect ways of delaying or refusing to cooperate with others or to work. For example, the following reasons can be given: work overload, too-tight schedule, team size, unbalanced composition of the team in terms of personnel, unwillingness of one's own superior to let them collaborate. There are no limits to the spirit of invention.

## 3.4 Resistance as a Game of Rivalry

Resistance can be seen as a game of rivalry when one person or group takes a stand against another person or group, thereby competing with other beliefs, perspectives, values, approaches, or solutions. Competition can be experienced as invigorating, inspiring, or inciting. Let's take an example from the world of soccer. For years, Lionel Messi and Cristiano Ronaldo have been in constant competition with each other. It's all about goals, trophies, titles, or individual awards. Cristiano Ronaldo admits that the rivalry is part of his life. But he also adds: "It's not true that we have a bad relationship. We are colleagues and have a professional relationship." And: "We have to take this rivalry in a positive way because it's a good thing. I hope we can both laugh about it all." This rivalry is a "good thing" because it spurs on ever better performances, but of course also because it generates media attention, brings money, and highlights the market value of the two top scorers.

Competition or rivalry can be experienced or acted out in very different ways. This depends very much on how the two parties perceive each other. Do I see the other person as an imaginative and powerful opponent who inspires me to come up with new ideas and thus energizes my actions and aspirations? Or as an incompetent weakling who is not to be taken seriously? Or as my worst enemy, who threatens my integrity or position and therefore needs to be weakened or eliminated? In the following, managers explain that resistance arises from rivalry. No matter how it is justified, the result is a prolonged antagonism that confronts them as a hard, insurmountable reality. So, what does this have to do with resistance? The actual source of resistance in these cases is always the other side. It is seen as the cause that triggers the rivalry and fires it up again and again.

Rivalry games were also mentioned in the previous chapter. At this point, however, it is not about an open power struggle, but about a covert or subtle struggle for authority and the preservation of authority. In the following case, the superior is out to secure his position. A divisional head at a hospital said his superior generally likes his ideas. He usually has a free hand and can make decisions and then implement them himself. He greatly appreciates this freedom, but notes that his superior has a problem with it as soon as the higher management level comes into play:

*"He showed resistance when, for example, the management or another higher authority had to be brought on board to decide on principles. His problem was that the idea didn't come from him. So, he balked. Fighting this resistance was always very difficult."*

He explains the unruly reaction from the superior's understanding of management, which could read as follows: I am legitimized as a manager when ideas and concerns from my area of responsibility are attributed exclusively to me by the superior. In this logic, the managers must feel that they are the cause, otherwise they lose their legitimacy as managers. As soon as the manager has the impression that their employees are claiming causality for themselves ("I invented it and not you"), they feel robbed of their causality and see a threat to their legitimacy.

The divisional manager sums up that it was an uphill struggle. Rivalries can develop into endless unproductive but also painful dynamics. One such case is described by a young manager from the sports industry at the time of the experience. The young man worked in a company that was merged with another company. He was one of the very few employees to transfer to the new organization. He then officially became a member of the extended management team and, as Head of Retail, was responsible for training programs, store construction, external profiling, and business consulting for retailers. His boss was the CEO. During the takeover talks, he was promised a lot in terms of personnel, budget, and personal responsibility. But the reality turned out quite differently:

> *"I was on my own, was given neither a budget nor staff, and the tasks were constantly being redefined. The CEO often needed me as a sparring partner in discussions about the further development of the company, a new organizational structure, strategic directions and so on. This culminated in me developing two or three scenarios for the future of the company."*

In day-to-day business, however, he increasingly felt that he no longer had access to the CEO and was being cut off from information. Before the summer vacation, he then requested a further meeting to define the framework for the coming months and clarify his role in the future organization. The CEO's intentions quickly became clear during the meeting:

*"The CEO explained to me that the Board of Directors had now decided on a new strategy with a new organization and presented me with one of my own proposals, so to speak. However, the word 'vacant' was written next to my own position. He then explained to me full-on that I could, for example, take over the training division within my previous small department ... as it was strategically extremely important ... under a new department head."*

The message was immediately clear to the narrator:

*"I offered my resignation during this conversation and left the company around six months later. I licked those wounds for a long time, as this was my first professional setback, and it really dented my ego. There could be several reasons for this resistance. The chemistry between the CEO and me was certainly not right, we were too different types. I was subsequently told by people close to the CEO that I had become too much of a competitor for him internally – but we are in the midst of hypotheses here."*

From the manager's point of view, the CEO repeatedly and systematically fails to keep his promises. In addition to this lack of reliability, the CEO also uses his Head of Retail for his own purposes and ultimately demotes him with the aim of getting rid of him. The manager resists him and puts up resistance to a young up-and-coming manager. From the manager's point of view, the CEO triggered the rivalry and practiced it continuously. The young Head of Retail sees himself as a committed, competent, and creative young manager and at the mercy of the rivalry game due to his hierarchical subordination. At the moment of de facto demotion, he is no longer willing to put up with this. The suspicions were validated. In this game of rivalry, he sees no possibility of changing the game; instead, he himself becomes a victim of this game of rivalry. He decides that he no longer wants to be the other person's pawn and frees himself from the situation by quitting.

## 3.5 Resistance as Personal Rejection

"I don't agree with what you're saying!" We can usually live with such a statement if we grant the other person the right to an independent opinion or at least accept it. After all, this is about the matter at hand. It is a different matter if the "whole person" is not accepted and is rejected. In psychology, it is assumed that people are afraid of rejection and can cause or reinforce this feeling in themselves or others through distorted self-perception (Vorauer et al. 2003). In managers' accounts of resistance situations, there are relatively frequent stories in which managers experience resistance as personal rejection by others. I assume that managers are not fundamentally deficient or even ill-disposed. I simply see personal rejection as a form of resistance. A divisional manager of a hospital reports that a team member was chosen as foreman because he "impressed" through excellent work performance and a positive work attitude. After the managers involved in the recruitment process had held various discussions with the candidate, they agreed that he should become the new foreman. However, the divisional manager was very surprised by the reaction of the other team members:

> *"After the decision was announced to the group members, the intrigues began. The resistance took the form of pure jealousy. They worked against him, and various conversations became necessary. The work colleagues became an enemy. Because they took it personally that he, not they, had been chosen. The foreman was under constant observation by his employees and had to perform even better. Every decision he made was scrutinized to the hilt. At some point, the dust settled. After a few weeks, he was accepted because the employees saw that he was really working for the service and not against them."*

In this case, the employees deprive the person of the legitimacy of being a manager at all. From the divisional manager's point of view, the rejection is only directed against the person. How is this rejection motivated? From the divisional manager's point of view, it can be attributed to "base motives" (envy, jealousy) on the part of the employees. However, there could very well be other coherent explanations, such as the employees having a proxy conflict with the foreman, which should be fought out with the line manager (the narrator). It is also conceivable that there are factual differences relating to the foreman. Or the resistance is an expression of a long-standing rivalry. These are certainly just speculations. I am not mentioning them here to replace old speculations with new ones, but rather to show that there may be completely different interpretations and backgrounds that the manager is not aware of in the specific situation. The new foreman has to prove that he is a good supervisor for the team. However, he succeeds in overcoming the rejection. It happens again and again that managers are elected and the reaction to the election is not as expected. In this case, however, the explanations end a little too quickly with the negative and deficient characteristics of the employees. It might have helped to make the situation bearable for the new manager if the background to the rejection had been explored in more detail.

In the following case, a young manager in the sports sector is also confronted with a personal rejection. After graduating, the person concerned worked for two years at one of the major management consultancies. He then moved to a sports retailer. He replaced a purchasing manager who was made redundant at the age of 58. He was aware that he was half the age of his predecessor, had an academic background, and was working in an environment that was hardly academic. His team consisted of employees of the same age, all of whom had an education in sports or communications and a lot of professional experience. He described the customers as seasoned, experienced corporate pioneers with their own sports businesses. At first glance, very differently socialized groups came together. The manager attributed the resistance in the team to one person:

*"In the team itself, there was above all a hardware buyer of the same age who was extremely critical of me and constantly tested me, as he had raised his own hopes for this job. This manifested itself in minor rebukes, a somewhat know-it-all demeanor, carrying out his own activities with not always clear agreements, etc. The resistance was therefore rather insidious, covert, never completely transparent, but enormously energy-sapping and grueling, especially as this was my first management position in the private sector and I was still searching for my own management style after around two years of military training."*

The hardware buyer of the same age resigned after around a year. But the grueling management situation was also evident in external relations: there was a lack of acceptance amongst the customers, the sports retailers. The manager attributed this to various reasons: the sports retailers were the same age as his predecessor, which meant that the age difference was very wide, and he belonged to a different generation. In this respect, too, he clearly lacked professional experience in the sports industry. After all, the sports retailers were personal friends with the predecessor, who had been insensitively retired from the company. It was hard to imagine how the personal rejection could be overcome. Chance helped:

*"This became noticeable during a ski testing exercise around five months after starting work. When I arrived on site as a representative of our organization, I was asked shortly afterwards by three older specialist retailers to ski a freeride variant with them. This was less of a friendly invitation and more of an obvious test and assessment for the young academic theorist. As I had passed my professional exam to become a ski instructor a few years earlier, I was fortunately able to hold my own. After the first trip, I was offered the German 'Du'*

*form of 'you,' was invited for another trip and a Kafi Lutz,[1] and
I have had full recognition within this group ever since."*

The former purchasing manager summarizes that his ability
to ski had nothing to do with his job. This also makes it clear that
the personal rejection is aimed directly at the person, not at their
abilities, attitudes, or other aspects of the person. It doesn't matter
what the person does or fails to do; they are completely rejected as
a person without further examination or assessment. This rejection
can lead to them being played, ostracized, picked out, or trashed.
The sports retailers' negative images of him as a person are unal-
terable and could be as follows: "He is a theoretician and therefore
can't understand anything about practice," "He is the beneficiary of
the unjustified dismissal of a colleague we value," "He doesn't know
the industry," "He is an aloof, arrogant consultant who doesn't want
to get his fingers dirty," "He doesn't smell right." This means that
he has an enormous number of characteristics that show that he
doesn't belong. He is kept at a distance, picked out and ostracized
from the close-knit community of like-minded people. By chance,
however, he is then able to prove the opposite. He has a crucial skill
(skiing), which he can demonstrate without imposing himself and
thus instantly soften the rigid ideas. He succeeds in proving himself
to be one of them without having intended or staged it.

The resistance that manifests itself in a personal rejection is
not simply a dimension in the relationship, but a decisive one.
The person is rejected as a whole or completely and will then
be unable to achieve anything in the matter. This leads to the
conclusion that acceptance of the person is fundamental to the
legitimacy of the manager. If this acceptance is lacking, legitimacy
cannot be achieved. A rejection on merit can be countered if the
person themselves is accepted.

---

[1] ... or Luzerner Kafi, Kafi Zwetschgen, Kaffee Träsch, Kaffee fertig. This is a Swiss national drink. It consists
of thin coffee flavored with sugar and pome fruit schnapps and served in a coffee glass.

## 3.6 Resistance as Willful Damage to the Organization

Whilst resistance in the previous chapter is shown in the lack of acceptance and the resulting rejection of the person, we will now turn to resistance as willful destruction. This involves deliberate, usually covert actions or omissions that impair, damage, or even destroy an aspect of the workplace environment. These actions can be directed against property, products, services, processes, or the reputation of the organization. Ultimately, acts of destruction undermine the goals of management (Taylor and Walton 1971). The damage is intended to make a statement. For example, a construction worker reported how he and some other colleagues let management know that they were angry at not receiving the promised pay rise (Tucker 1993, p. 36):

> "We maltreated our tools until they broke, or we bought more materials from the hardware store in town than we actually needed, and we kept a few things for ourselves, like small tools, pieces of hose, timber etc. We believed that if we increased the cost and reduced the profit of the work, the president would get the message loud and clear."

States also sabotage. Cyber weapons are becoming a tool for international conflicts. It is suspected that the United States and Israel developed malware called Stuxnet to manipulate the Iranian nuclear program. It is considered a masterpiece of programming. Stuxnet was infiltrated into the control systems and recorded the scheduled processes in the centrifuges that enrich the uranium. These recordings were then played to the inspectors in a continuous loop, while the running speed of the centrifuges was changed in the background, thus sabotaging uranium enrichment (Langer 2014, p. 1).

In organizations, deliberate damage is certainly not only caused by employees on the front line, but also by managers and technocrats (LaNuez and Jermier 1994). These are usually acts that take place in anonymity and can give rise to all kinds of suspicions. Let us take the introduction of free-kick pitch sprays in soccer as a current illustrative example. The German testing company TÜV assessed the spray and concluded that the product was "not marketable in its current form in Germany and the EU." Amongst other things, "parabens were found that are suspected of having a hormonal effect." In addition, the "labels on the product are inadequate, incomplete, and not in German." The inventor of the spray, Brazilian Heine Allemagne, reacted to this decision with the following words:

> *"The spray has been used in several countries and thousands of soccer matches in recent years without any problems. But I suspected that something like this would happen. (…) I'm not crazy enough to produce something harmful. I believe in sabotage. Maybe the TÜV got tampered cans, maybe someone is trying to blacken our name?"*

The spray bottle was relabeled, further tests followed with positive results, and finally DEKRA, a testing company that competes with TÜV, certified that the spray was harmless. The spray was used for the first time in German professional soccer on October 17, 2014.

Was there sabotage? Did someone accuse someone else? Was damage intended? The story reported in the media remains opaque to outsiders. Without knowing the exact circumstances, the test reports, and the exchanges between experts and counter-experts, the observer is left with nothing but persistent, sometimes entertaining, speculation but no certainty. The guesswork about the causes, who did what, and motives can begin. But if there is no evidence, there is only conjecture. Such stories are also great material for conspiracy theories, scandals, and attempts to cover up these very scandals. Let's take a closer look at this in the following case study.

A new IT system was to be introduced at a US Health Maintenance Organization (HMO), a healthcare provider (Prasad and Prasad 2000). The HMO employed physicians, nurses, junior doctors, radiologists, dietitians, receptionists, managers, and office staff. Due to the takeover of the HMO by a larger healthcare company called Superior, a change in organizational culture became apparent. The employees feared that the family atmosphere and interpersonal closeness could be lost. The pace of work had also increased slightly. Employees also mentioned that different expectations were clashing, collaboration had become noticeably more formal, and tension had increased. In addition, a new managing director had recently taken over at HMO, who was described by HMO employees as a "true Superior type." It was announced that many administrative functions were to be converted to data processing. Previously, all administrative tasks had been performed manually. After a few months, three senior nurses and an attending nurse carried out most of the training under the direction of Superior's project manager. At the same time, the staff were able to familiarize themselves with the use of computers in their daily work on test screens. The system then went online, and all scheduling, invoicing, and records were processed electronically.

To talk about the wanton destruction, it makes sense to place it in the context of the events, and so the immediate reactions to the IT introduction are reported first. Most employees could not imagine the exact nature of the technological change and were understandably concerned about the impact on their activities and the transformation of their work. This concern came up from time to time but was not heard in the training seminars or meetings. Employees were also dissatisfied with the seminars as they felt they did not provide them with enough information and left employees confused about the actual technical operation. Reactions to the system finally installed varied from joy and reconciliation to suspicion and hostility. The managers were fully convinced of the functionality, whereas the employees were much more ambivalent about the impact on their day-to-day work. It was reported within the organization that, from the managers' point of view, the introduction had gone smoothly. There were no formal protests or collective opposition, but a closer look revealed everyday, informal acts of resistance. In the seminars, for example, questions were repeatedly asked about health (i.e. whether the repetitive movements at the keyboard could cause injuries to hands, or whether there was a connection between miscarriages or damage to a fetus and working at a computer). The answers given by the trainers did not satisfy the questioners:

> *"I think ... it was pretty clear to all of us that she had very little awareness about any of this."*

At the beginning, resistance was expressed in that the immediate decision (i.e. the introduction of computers) was seemingly casually questioned in the seminars. Because the real or pretended doubts about the health consequences were not taken up by the management and there was no discussion of them at management level, the legitimacy of the decision and thus also of the management began to wane. According to the implicit criticism, the management had failed to consider the far-reaching health consequences – a cardinal error on the part of the management from the employees' point of view, which should not have occurred in a healthcare company.

In another case, a receptionist insisted on the old system even though her supervising nurse repeatedly warned her that her behavior was unacceptable. The receptionist calmly listened to the warnings and returned to her manual method as soon as her supervisor was out of sight. After a few days, the supervisor sternly admonished the receptionist, saying that she was:

*"tired of dealing with ignorant women who could not appreciate the value of computers."*

The receptionist replied, just as pointedly, that her reluctance to give up the old method was not because she didn't appreciate computers, but because she claimed the right to make the change gradually. In the absence of her superiors, she said to her colleagues:

*"Management always takes its own time to make decisions about anything but expects us to dance to their own tunes at once. Well, we need a bit more practice to dance to the new tune. And if they don't give me the time, I'll take it anyway."*

Those in charge dismissed other similar behavior as complaining or described it as "foolish," "silly," or "hysterical." With this assessment, employees no longer had to be taken seriously from a management perspective. For some employees, on the other hand, sticking to manual work was an expression of resistance to the enormous speed of technological change. However, it was not a question of maintaining their habits, but of asserting their right to control their own working rhythm and countering management expectations. In this case, the employees did not show a lack of insight, but consciously resisted, although management did not describe this as resistance. Employees only made themselves heard by "speaking like the management" (i.e. by pointing out specific, functional software problems). Only then did the line managers consider other arguments such as health problems.

Other actions were then labeled as resistance, although it is noticeable here that individuals never identified themselves with any of the actions but attributed them to other known or unknown employees. Before the official introduction of the computers, a number of brand-new video display terminals (VDTs) were delivered and stored in a storeroom in the basement of the building. Shortly after the VDTs were delivered, the basement was flooded due to an alleged accident, an age-related burst pipe. After a short time, this flooding was interpreted by the managers and the rest of the workforce as a deliberate act of sabotage to delay or thwart the fitting of computers to the work-stations. Employees said they were unaware that there were such "perverts" in the organization capable of such a thing and expressed anger at this vile act of sabotage. Others spoke of "our own IRA job" and speculated as to who was responsible. In time, everyone assumed it was a deliberate act of sabotage. IT adminis-trators joked that they now had to deal with a "real guerrilla war" and that "gas masks" were now part of the new uniform. Later, managers, staff, and doctors spoke of a clever act of sabotage that delayed the introduction of the computers for several weeks and cost the Superior group thousands of dollars.

The decisive factor for this incident being interpreted as a (clever) act of sabotage is that willful intent was assumed. The firm conviction grew that the damage was caused deliberately. The cause of this damage could not really be clearly and unequiv-ocally attributed to human manipulation, let alone to a specific person or group of people. There was obviously no evidence that it was such a destructive act, but the interpretation of "sabotage" became entrenched and an unquestioned certainty for everyone.

This and other examples indicate that the suspected sabotage is not an irrational act by dissatisfied employees who mutate into mad and crazy saboteurs. The actions are rather rational, con-spiratorial, but also calculated and thus restrained behaviors that have a high symbolic value (Jermier 1988). The actors weigh up the negative risks (exposure, exclusion, criminal liability) against the positive consequences (changes in their own interests or in the interests of colleagues, the organization, and society) (LaNuez and Jermier, 1994, p. 221).

In the HMO organization, however, managers then explicitly identified other employee behaviors as resistance. This involved minor damage caused by employees. For example, employees left half-full coffee cups or Pepsi cans next to the computer, which were then regularly knocked over by someone else. Or they "forgot" to switch off the computer in the evening or to save data, or they stuck chewing gum on the screen. Managers described these behaviors as "careful carelessness," as no willful intent could be proven, only carelessness or thoughtlessness. Employees accepted or took responsibility for the negligence, as opposed to the subversive acts that severely impacted the economic well-being of the organization. Management was certain that even the minor damage was deliberate, planned, and calculated. From this point of view, it couldn't be any different if you put one and one together. However, these were merely assumptions on the part of the management. It could either have been an accumulation of carelessness, as the employees were clearly untrained in using a technical device at work. Or it could have been a case of unconscious negligence resulting from a growing detachment and decreasing identification with the organization as a whole.

What effect did the acts of sabotage have beyond the immediate damage and destruction of working capital? We need to tell the story of the suspected deliberate act of sabotage a little further. During the flood, suspicion fell on Janet, an experienced nurse and fierce critic of most management strategies. She was considered an "old troublemaker" by managers. Managers also admitted to being intimidated by her caustic wit and quick uptake. Janet was never considered popular, even amongst her trusted colleagues, because of her sarcasm. That changed with the incident. She was seen as the saboteur and thus received universal admiration from the employees. She was described as "courageous" because she was "willing to teach management a lesson." Janet neither confirmed nor denied this attribution.

The suspected act of sabotage creates a "heroine of the workplace" and thus a tangible symbol of resistance in the organization. In the eyes of some other employees, the heroism of one employee symbolizes the fact that the employees do not simply tacitly agree with the management's decisions. The act of sabotage becomes a kind of self-encouragement for the workforce, which gradually loses control over key aspects of its work. This incident also affects authority. If it is an accident, the authority of the management is not affected, but as soon as the incident is classified as an act of sabotage, it exposes the vulnerability of the management.

Managers, in turn, became increasingly frustrated and nervous as they were unable to allocate blame for the alleged accidents or mistakes, revealing their inability to control the behavior of certain employees. As a result, management was keen to reduce acts of sabotage or resistance of any kind. They tried to appease employees through informal measures: turning a blind eye to tardiness, ignoring errors on time sheets, allowing employees to leave work slightly earlier than normal, introducing more flexible work schedules, etc. Managers were aware that such measures were necessary to ensure the smooth functioning of work processes.

Willful destruction can, as in this case, manifest itself in direct action. Company property (such as machinery, office equipment, operating facilities), data, or products and services are damaged or destroyed. However, it can also take place more subtly, with people behaving in a way that causes damage against typically better judgment. For example, quality controls can be ordered or carried out carelessly; critical information can be withheld; or destructive and damaging behavior by employees can be deliberately overlooked, approved, or accepted. However, the organization can also be deliberately damaged by statements; by leaking confidential information to competitors; or by denigrating the organization, its services, or products in front of customers. It can also happen that managers make disparaging remarks about the company to employees with the aim of impairing productivity through lower satisfaction, higher absenteeism, or fluctuation (LaNuez and Jermier 1994, pp. 240–243).

But how do people come to display such destructive behavior? The behavior may be aimed at change: something is to be prevented, power relations that are perceived as too hierarchical are to be balanced out, injustices are to be rectified or, as in the case above, control over one's own activity and work situation is to be regained. However, destructive behaviors can also be aimed at better coping with the perceived work situation: defense of entitlements, expression of frustration or resignation, or simply a satisfaction of having gotten back at "the system" (LaNuez and Jermier 1994, p. 244).

But whatever may be behind the willful destruction, it is crucial not to simply dismiss it as a base act of sabotage by malicious delinquents, but to investigate how it could have happened. The HMO was caught in a destructive spiral and realized that it had to be generous to its employees to slowly find its way out of the negative spiral.

Sabotage can also be related to an employee feeling unfairly treated and not being listened to, for example, a temporary employee in the warehouse of a retail store received less salary than others in similar positions. After an unsuccessful attempt to discuss this with his supervisor, he decided to deal with the matter in his own way (Tucker 1993, p. 37):

> "I didn't want to just quit, so I lazed around a lot. I didn't do anything unless I was told to. When I worked nights, I would listen to music for hours and do nothing. When I was lazing around and saw the manager, I pretended I was actually doing something."

It would now be easy to conclude that strict compliance regulations should be drawn up, adherence to them demanded, and sanctions threatened to prevent such destructive acts. If we look at the case study outlined above and see the behavior as an expression of organizational resistance, then it is not simply a matter of avoiding and preventing damaging behavior. Rather, the task of management is to shape the organization in such a way that the behavioral tendency toward wanton destruction is not encouraged. If such destruction does occur, not all employees should be placed under general suspicion and repressive measures should not be taken immediately to prevent further misconduct. Rather, the task of management is to better understand what is behind the actions and what, if any, justifiable reasons lie behind the unjustified actions.

## Summary

- Resistance is not only obvious but can also be covert. However, such resistance is by no means simply ineffective.

- Covert resistance refers to a distancing from the organization or from a specific person and manifests itself in humor, games of rivalry, submissive actions, sophisticated refusals, but also in acts of destruction.

- Covert resistance points to dysfunctionalities, problems, or differences of opinion and is capable of delaying, thwarting, or dismantling the plans of others (management, superiors, colleagues, employees).

# 4

# Repressed Resistance

I don't need a friend who changes when I change and who
nods when I nod; my shadow does that much better.
                    —Plutarch (c. 45–125 CE), Greek philosopher

In the previous two chapters, we have seen resistance as loud or
quiet, open or hidden, effective or ineffective. When resistance is
repressed, we primarily assume that resistance within a hierarchy
is suppressed. To illustrate this, I would like to quote from the
novel *Between the Palaces* by Nagib Machfus, as I did at the beginning of the book. Abd al-Gawwad is the father of a Cairo merchant
family whose life and daily routine are described in detail in the
novel. Outside the family, Abd al-Gawwad is regarded as a kind
friend, generous businessman, witty entertainer, connoisseur of
art, and, finally, a sensitive lover of beautiful women. He forbids
his family members all the pleasures and excesses that he allows
himself. He believes that strictness, discipline, and order keep the
family together. He demands obedience and tolerates no dissent.

In the family, he becomes an overbearing, merciless patriarch. His wife and children love and respect him for his religious principles and ideals. At the same time, they fear him. But even if there is no open contradiction, the family members seek and find their freedoms, which are strictly forbidden by their father. But under no circumstances must this come to their father's attention, because if it does, he punishes the offense with relentless severity. His second eldest son, Fahmi, reflects on this when he has an argument with his father about his active role in the demonstrations and strikes for the end of the British protectorate (Machfus 1996, p. 585 et seq.):

> *"Why didn't he promise his father to be obedient and then do what he thought was right? In this house, lying was not shameful, because no one could live peacefully in their father's shadow if they did not protect themselves with lies. When people were among themselves, they talked about it openly, and in times of need they even talked to each other. (...) Nobody shied away from it, because if they always told their father the truth, life would be unbearable."*

This scene takes place almost a 100 years ago in a different culture from our own. The young man's reflection beautifully illustrates that although the despotic ruler believes he leads his subjects through life like puppets on the strings of his unrestricted power, they know how to evade his influence, even if they love and adore their father above all else. The resistance takes place quietly, as undetected as possible in the shadow of the father's sphere of influence. The despot has the upper hand and overthrowing the situation is not impossible, but the possibilities of influence are distributed completely differently. Nevertheless, the subordinates resist, but they do so as unnoticed as possible. This is not repressed resistance, but covert resistance. The scene depicted has certain parallels to everyday working life, as there are indeed management relationships in which it is clear to everyone involved that opposition is unwelcome: "The boss doesn't like to hear that sort of thing," "You'd better not say anything – you don't know whether you'll get a warning if you do." There is no open resistance because the employees obey or at least give the impression that they are obeying. They do everything they can to avoid being caught if they do not comply with instructions.

However, resistance can really be repressed in organizations. This does not require a patriarch or despot, but rather "the organization" itself brings it about that "resistance is resisted." To illustrate this, we will take a closer look at the internal mechanisms of a company from the business and management consulting sector, Magnum Consulting (Kärreman and Alvesson 2009), where employees follow the organization's prevailing norms without coercion or pressure, thereby suppressing resistance.

People working in the consulting industry are considered knowledge workers who willingly submit to extreme working conditions, such as very long working hours or extensive travel. The tasks are complex and are managed by highly qualified employees through a high degree of self-organization. They must constantly apply their stock of knowledge, methods, and solutions to new, unstructured starting situations. In these companies, employees rarely engage in protests or sabotage and very few signs of more subtle forms of resistance are visible. Where does this power that largely prevents resistance come from?

Magnum Consulting is a fast-growing, global management consultancy with 30 000 employees. Around 70% of employees are under 30 years old. The principle of career orientation applies. Employees are expected to progress from analyst or consultant to manager to partner on a fixed timetable. Only a small number succeed in the latter. Younger employees monitor their position in the management consultancy's promotion system very closely. Magnum presents itself completely differently from the idealized image of a contemporary, future-oriented company, which, one might assume, is attractive to today's young people. This is because Magnum has a hierarchical structure, and the company has systems, structures, and procedures for almost everything. Magnum is therefore more like a traditional bureaucracy. The company attaches great importance to employees behaving obediently and conforming to standards. The hierarchy stands for the constant increase in competence that every committed employee strives for continuously and in competition with others: "up or out." The hierarchy is not primarily an expression of distance, antagonism, or alienation, but nourishes the constant pursuit of personal career goals.

New employees begin to identify with Magnum very quickly, unreservedly, and strongly, because – and this is repeatedly emphasized by HR during the induction phase – the novices have chosen this type of work themselves. New employees are recruited at the top end of the job market, there are programs for ongoing skills development, salaries are extremely high, and career prospects are excellent. Magnum employees consider themselves to be part of the elite, which gives them status and a high sense of self-worth. The focus is not on individual development, nor is it primarily about being as creative or spontaneous as possible. The individual, especially at the lower levels of the hierarchy, is ultimately interchangeable. The company is not dependent on them. The company's main resource lies in its structures, methods, and regulations, so that it is not dependent on the abilities of the individual. Community, cooperation, and conformity are therefore emphasized. Conformity is of great importance, as advisors are confronted with complex and unstructured problem situations in the course of their work and are constantly having to make discretionary decisions. This means that they are not easy to control. In this

context, it is even more important that their work is highly reliable, predictable, and efficient. This in turn requires professional
distance, but also rational thinking and reasoning. After all, everyone must have their emotions under control.

Even though Magnum is an attractive employer, there are
also various concerns on the part of employees. One consultant,
for example, answers the question of what customers expect
from her:

> "That I, as a consultant, have answers to all questions. That's my
> experience so far. That I am the expert I have to be sold as. That I
> quickly can build confidence in my capabilities. To deliver, to always be
> around. Always. You are an around-the-clock slave, and you are not
> expected to have a life outside work."

Even when, as in this case, negative elements of the work
are discussed, there is hardly any resistance. This can be attributed to the fact that certain principles are firmly anchored in the
self-image of consultants: The work is hard, is done ambitiously,
and is delivered on time. Appropriate skills are a prerequisite but
are also constantly being developed. This is rewarded with good
career opportunities and promotions. Today, however, there are
also clearly conflicting ideas about how work can be organized.
Just think of the demand for a good work-life balance or autonomy in terms of the content or timing of work. Both logics are
at least potentially contradictory. If consultants do not adhere to
the expected norms of the consulting firm, they become devi-
ants. If, on the other hand, they completely subordinate themselves to the work, they become "slaves of the company" and
lose autonomy.

Where does the fundamental or potential contradiction
lead, or how do the advisors themselves deal with it? There are
various conspicuous reaction patterns here. On the one hand, the

potentially negative is turned into a positive, as demonstrated by a project manager:

> *"It is simply impossible not to be carried away by the enthusiasm, the feeling that this must simply be done, although we are only five when we ought to be 10. You must go on, and to start back-pedalling in that situation, to say that I don't want to do this, that's just unthinkable."*

Enthusiasm seduces, carries away, and pushes aside possible doubts, but also the possibility that doubts could be expressed seriously or get out of hand. In addition, it is considered an incontrovertible, non-negotiable fact that you simply have to work hard and all the time. Even young consultants have internalized this immediately:

> *"I worked a lot on weekends when I started to work here. I think that's natural. Everyone at Magnum wants to demonstrate their worth. We are often very driven, so you automatically work weekends when you are a freshman, and when there is a need. My reason for working weekends was that I wanted to reach a level of understanding and competence that felt comfortable. And I think that most want to reach that level as soon as possible. Which is good for the company, because when you have self-confidence, others are confident about you."*

There are no signs of resistance here, simply because the working conditions are described as completely normal. Others report that they have now learned to appreciate their free time and the time before their job much more, because back then they only really had free time and freedom. Even here, something positive is wrested from the enormous workload, as the possibility of having gained insight and a learning experience as a result. And even if individual consultants have slight doubts as to whether the work culture itself is good or good for them, there is no way of questioning or criticizing it. At the very moment that resistance to work norms and the work culture begins to shine through, the principles take effect and override the resistance. Reality is harsh, irrevocable. It is what it is. You have to accept it, but without wallowing in resignation, sinking into self-pity, or even expressing criticism within the organization. The strong norms of the company work: you have to accept the obvious negatives and enthusiastically find something positive in them.

Resistance does not occur in this example, but this is not caused by the positional power of superiors or their direct and continuous influence, but rather by the fact that the members of the organization have internalized the guiding principles so strongly that it is inconceivable to think beyond them or question them. The norms of the corporate culture are self-evident; there is no need for any interaction, no need for a superior, no need for clarification; everyone simply knows how things work here. The culture of the company becomes an impregnable fortress. The system is – quite obviously – economically successful and attracts highly competent young employees, but it is just as rigid and immunizes itself against any change in working conditions.

## Summary

- There are conditions in organizations that lead to resistance being repressed.

- The suppression of resistance occurs without the intervention of people, such as a dominant superior, but simply through the guidelines for action working in the background, which every member of the organization has adopted and internalized at the beginning of their employment.

- Organizations in which resistance is repressed are strongly oriented toward conformity. For the members of the organization, it is simply unthinkable to question the existing norms.

# 5

# Shortcut Assumptions That Lead to a Dead End

The life that most people lead shows them until they realize it clearly: you can also run your head into open doors.

—Erich Kästner

The diversity of resistance is evident in the forms of resistance described in the previous chapters. We have now become familiar with three different groupings: in the case of *overt resistance*, which cannot be overlooked, disputes take place between specific individuals or groups of people. There are often concrete demands on the table. This resistance is experienced by those involved as (very) confrontational. In the case of *covert resistance*, the subject matter automatically becomes more diffuse, so it becomes unclear what it is about, what exactly the resistance is directed against, who or even whether anyone is resisting at all, and how to react to the resistance, if it exists at all. It is even more difficult to recognize the resistance, to understand its origin and to trace it back to specific individuals or groups. With *repressed resistance*, overt resistance can be suppressed, but hidden forms of resistance can still occur underground within the organization. In the case of repressed resistance, it does not require the positional power of the management to repress resistance. This is done by the norms learned and internalized by all members of the organization. They ensure that the organization enjoys extensive protection against the resistance virus.

Let us remind ourselves once again that situations associated with resistance are perceived as exceptions. They appear unexpectedly, unsettle, irritate, stir up emotions, or make people angry. The person experiencing resistance, but also the person creating resistance, often no longer have their emotions under control, but try to control them. Because something is at stake here. For example, the resistance is directed against a decision that the person being attacked has made or is partly responsible for. The person who made the decision feels exposed, criticized, attacked, or even fundamentally questioned. Resistance challenges the other person, the hierarchy. From the point of view of the resistor, things look a little different. It is not without its challenges to put up resistance, because the individual exposes themselves and takes a risk. You simply don't know exactly how the other side will react: will the people concerned take the demand seriously? Will I be ostracized or cut off in the future? Will I be putting my career goals at risk?

No matter what forms of resistance we talk about, it usually expresses the fact that the management, or whoever the resistance is directed against, does not have the resistors under control (quite as hoped). This exceptional situation is unsettling. At such moments, all those involved leave the safe terrain and move onto sandy ground. Far from the usual, expected reactions, everyone involved wonders how they should behave and how the other person will react to what they have just done or said. It is impossible to predict exactly. You are not immune to unpleasant surprises, but there can also be surprisingly positive effects. In some situations, there is also the fact that you can't just sit back and let things pass you by. A reaction, a response, is imminent and is usually expected to happen quickly.

However, uncertainty also arises from the fact that it is often not entirely clear what is at stake and where the resistance is coming from. When demands are made clearly and authentically or a whistleblower acts against the organization, the actors are clearly identifiable. But here too, the question arises as to whether others are not feeling the same way, whether there is something brewing in the team, the department, or the entire organization without the manager or management knowing about it.

Obviously, resistance situations are far from being easy to handle. They are diffuse, and it is difficult to penetrate their inner logic. In many cases, it can be observed that managers tend to give quick, hasty, and conclusive reasons. These justifications are based on assumptions that are no longer questioned and are deeply rooted in the person's self-image. These are "only" models, but people assume that these models "really" represent reality (Senge 1990), when they are nothing more than products of our thinking. Reality is not simply present, but we create this reality (Dent and Goldberg 1999, p. 39, or Gergen 1999). One's own imagination or perception is therefore not reality, but simply a way of seeing things. Someone may present their view of reality completely convincingly and have many followers for it. It may also be a basis for (economic) success. But that doesn't make it true or correct. It is just a way of looking at things and a way of achieving success.

We need to distance ourselves from the idea that someone – whoever – perceives things as they really are. Instead, we produce templates into which we categorize our observations. And it is precisely these templates or mental models that are then equated with reality, or one could also say: confused with it. There are alternatives to every point of view and every point of view has its blind spots and its sunny and dark sides, which need to be explored, weighed up, and reflected upon. But if these points of view seem simple and as long as the individual falls back on them as a matter of course, they elude intellectual penetration and access. The individual is then unable to actively decide to perceive situations in a fundamentally different way or to behave in situations in a fundamentally different way.

It is precisely these constructivist considerations that I take as my starting point in this chapter. Some self-evident assumptions can be found in the context of resistance in organizations, which are presented and reflected upon here. The presentation and reflection of such assumptions, which are no longer questioned, serve to examine them with a certain distance from everyday events and to think about alternative ways of seeing and behaving, which, where appropriate, can lead to a more productive approach to resistance.

So, what is the problem with the self-evident assumptions listed below? They do not allow us to get to the bottom of the resistance. They are quickly applied without a person getting a clearer picture of what is actually going on. This is called "jumping to conclusions," which relies on the next best, most obvious, explanation, the one that is familiar and plausible. Israeli American psychologist Daniel Kahneman uses the somewhat unwieldy term "WYSIATI" for such leaps of judgment: "What you see is all there is" or "Only what you know counts" (Kahneman 2011, p. 113). Of course, it is not the case that hasty conclusions or rules of thumb are questionable per se. They allow us to grasp the world quickly and experience ourselves as capable of acting. They can help in complex situations that require a quick decision, precisely because they hide information (Gigerenzer and Gaissmaier 2006; Gigerenzer 2008). I am therefore not questioning the functionality of all hasty conclusions. But I do question whether all hasty conclusions lead to a productive handling of resistance or a productive dynamic in organizations.

I refer to the mental explanation models presented below as shortcuts, because they shorten the path to knowledge and understanding. The explanations are already there before the resistance even arises because they are frequently repeated, common, and typical beliefs that are used and believed by many. I formulate them here as aphorisms (i.e. short, memorable sayings that claim to be universally valid). Most of the aphorisms can be found in individual stories and cases in the previous chapters, albeit in a different linguistic form. I therefore summarize the hastily made assumptions and conclusions in the titles and subtitles. Then I expand on them, sometimes exaggerating them a little to make their content clearer. Under the title "Taking alternative routes instead of shortcuts," I make suggestions as to how the reality of management can be seen and shaped differently.

It is important for me to make two things clear in advance: firstly, I have gained the impression from the interviews, research, and my own experience that these assumptions are widespread. However, I am not claiming that all managers make these assumptions. Secondly, in my opinion, it is in no way obvious or apparent how these shortcuts work and how they should be countered. At first glance, they may appear to be succinct formulations, but it should not be forgotten that they can also be helpful in coping with the complex day-to-day operations and management. I take them seriously, and this means that I try to understand them in more detail, to comprehend them and then to subject them to critical reflection. However, I would also like to invite the reader to come up with their own thoughts.

## 5.1 "People Are the Problem"

A very common assumption is that when resistance occurs, the problem or cause can be directly attributed to a person. In the descriptions and experiences of managers, this is reflected in the fact that resistance is prematurely attributed to a certain characteristic of people in general ("that's the way people are") or of a specific person ("that's obviously the way he/she is"). These may be characteristics or behaviors that, according to the assumption, are automatically triggered in all or very many people, especially in situations of change, and are therefore to be expected. Or they may be abnormal characteristics or behaviors because they are considered socially conspicuous, particularly disturbing, peculiar, exaggerated, or even pathological.

The attribution of causes of resistance to the person (i.e. personalization) (Ashforth and Mael 1998, p. 114), makes sense at first glance, because in everyday life we encounter people made of flesh and blood. We talk with people, whom we observe, with whom we deal, argue, or even just hear about. The special feature of characteristics is that they belong directly to the person, that they are deeply anchored in the person, are constantly expressed or are somehow triggered. The person is simply the way they are. Nothing can be done to change this, and no further explanation is required. This basic assumption is expressed in more detail in the following sentences.

### "People Only Do the Bare Minimum"

When it comes to change, managers often complain about very specific characteristics. One of these is a lack of willingness to change due to complacency, a lack of interest in development, insufficient commitment, or a general human tendency toward laziness. This offers managers an explanation, particularly for frustrating experiences in the organization, as in the following example of a manager from the food industry. As a young manager, he wanted to offer further training to 45 employees. The educational background of these people was very heterogeneous. The manager describes his experiences as follows:

> "*The company also supported this project. EQ training was organized at the appropriate level. However, the resistance of the secretarial and production staff was already enormous during the first training course. I had to realize that despite offering further training during working hours, there was no interest in this continuous offer. This resistance meant that the course for secretarial and production staff had to be canceled after the first module. I had to learn that these employees want to do their job from 08:00 to 16:00 and no longer!*"

In this story, the focus is on the manager's disappointment at the rejection of the offer, which is understandable at first glance. The manager probably found the offer attractive. However, there could be a whole host of other possible reasons for the employees' behavior, which could be related to the offer itself, the culture of the organization or past experiences with further training.

## "People Don't Want to Change"

In the previous section, employees are accused of not really being committed to the company, but of only focusing on their immediate tasks and duties. They lack motivation and a willingness to get involved. Another explanation is that employees generally find it difficult to have to give something up. One manager from the IT sector explains this as follows:

> "*I noticed that most of the resistance was about giving up personal habits. Comfort and respect in the event of change were often the biggest obstacles.*"

Employees, so the view goes, make themselves comfortable in the organization, no longer look for challenges, and try to make their everyday lives as pleasant as possible. However, it is not only the employees but also the management of an organization that can be considered lazy. Another manager, a department head from the IT sector, places the resistance on the CEO of the company. Although the CEO had given him the order to change, he himself did not immediately tackle the changes he felt were necessary:

> *"In the following two weeks, absolutely nothing happened. Meetings and customer visits took place in exactly the same way – as if there had never been a conversation about urgently needed changes."*

The idea is that people prefer to carry on with what they know and are familiar with. The "doers" clearly distance themselves from this. They have learned to overcome this natural, innate weakness, but always find themselves tied back by the inertia of other people.

## "They Are Just Naysayers"

According to some people, unwillingness can also take on an extreme form. It is not just a lack of motivation or drive that is assumed, but a systematic opposition. These naysayers block everything that deviates from the status quo and which expects them to try something new. Accordingly, they try to thwart all change. Without leaving the slightest doubt about his opinion, a video learning module by the long-celebrated management guru John Kotter cultivates the image of the typical naysayer, whose only interest is to boycott change:

> *"In a change process you will always find around you some people who basically always say: 'No, no.' And they really, strongly mean*

*that. These are the guys that resist to the death. We have a tendency to try to pull them in, to coopt them into the process, to work away and change their minds. And my tip is: Forget it. Get them out of the way, no matter who they are in terms of power or relationship to you. Because if you let them inside the tent, they will do so much damage that the change will be undermined. (...) My observation has been: If [the No-Nos] are strong enough it's hopeless. It's absolutely hopeless. And the only alternative you have is to get them out of the way, distract them, keep them out of the way. Because the mischief they can do is almost endless. The mischief for example ... and just smiling at you and saying 'yes, yes' but then going behind because you don't pay attention to them anymore and doing things that undo changes you've made. Talking to groups over here, saying: 'This is a little nuts.' And starting to win them over. Or promising to do something and then [saying]: 'Oh my gosh, I forgot' or 'I had this other priority.' It slows you down. (...) I think most of us do not like [to get them out of the way]. But I think in cases of significant change, when you've got the No-Nos around, that's the only solution. Really. The only solution."*

## "They're Just Scared"

Another characteristic observed in change processes is the assumption that people have an innate fear of change. It is difficult to do anything about this fear. The fear grows automatically once employees have become accustomed to the new. They would overcome the fear over time. The management then also tries to provide reassurance to reduce the fear. Sometimes, however, as in the case of the reorganization of the cantonal administration (see section 2.2), people are just a bit whiny or oversensitive. They shouldn't be like that; they should also recognize that management has to do its job. However, fear also serves as an explanation in the context of power games: for example, the head of marketing insinuates to the head of the bank (see section 2.1) that he is just "afraid of (...) a strike or something else" after all. Or the head of procurement, Regula, from the electricity industry explains that the head of the IT department is "afraid" of "losing his power" (see section 2.2). In other words, fear is seen as an explanation for cowardly, defensive, or aggressive, unfair behavior.

## "They Act Out of Base Motives"

However, members of the organization are also assumed to have base motives such as envy or jealousy, as is the case with the divisional manager in a hospital (see section 3.5). Base motives include, for example, a pronounced orientation toward one's own benefit or advantage, holding on to one's own sinecures and underhandedness, which are then often seen in connection with greed for power or obsession with power. We were able to observe this, in the case of the divisional manager and the head of department in the transport sector (see section 2.1) or in the description of Urs by Regula (see section 2.2). In the view of the whistleblower Anne (see section 2.3), the managers behaved so unscrupulously that they knowingly put human lives at risk and played this game of destruction for years. Anne also implicitly attributes this to base motives, which makes her morally indignant: "How can anyone be like this?" The person declared to be immoral thus loses their integrity and dignity. The base motives are seen as firmly anchored character traits of the person in question, which only deserve contempt and therefore no consideration. But here, too, we are dealing with attributions to the person. There could have been completely different, unknown group dynamics or organizational reasons guiding the actions.

## "They're Not Quite Right in the Head"

Let us now turn to ascribed attributes and characteristics that are serious and profound. Behaviors are attributed to private problems. Or people are said to be completely out of control, no longer ticking properly, no longer in control of themselves or making an extremely depressed impression. All these "findings" then serve as an explanation for or an expression of resistance, as we have seen in many cases in the previous chapters. This is not only psychologizing, but also pathologizing. The resistant behavior shows that the person is no longer able to work, perform, or work in a team. The behavior is then judged to be completely inappropriate or unpredictable. The behavior deviates greatly from the expected normal state and is considered pathological.

## "They Are to Blame"

We have now become familiar with various forms of psychologization. The resisters are attributed a lack of will or motivation, fear, obsession with power and deviousness, or psychological defects. The explanations have one thing in common. The explanation is conclusive and satisfying, and therefore no further reflection, questioning, or exploration is necessary. Through psychologization and pathologization, the other or others are conclusively evaluated and fixed to an unchangeable characteristic, as if one could see into the person and as if one were capable of such a judgment. This assumption has far-reaching consequences: fear must be reduced or accepted. Insidiousness can only be fought with insidiousness. If people lack the will, they have to be forced. If they are whiny, then they shouldn't put on airs; they must pull themselves together and obey. If they're in a bad mood, that's their problem. And if they show symptoms of illness, then they should go to the doctor, etc.

Let's go one step further. In the context of resistance, psychological and pathologizing attributions serve a specific purpose. We use these explanatory patterns because they bring us something, and we use these explanatory patterns quite automatically. We have previously established that psychologizing and pathologizing explanatory patterns have a conclusive effect, so the final reason seems to have been found, which is satisfying. Because an explanation suggests that you are right and that you can stick to what you intended to do. And it offers clarity, certainty, and therefore a good orientation for your own actions. But there is another useful effect: the cause of the resistance is exclusively and conclusively to be found in the other person or in the others. The other person is afraid, oversensitive, power-mad, or out of their mind, whereas we are completely healthy and behave appropriately. The characteristics, emotions, and behavioral dispositions are inherent in the other person or persons and are triggered by them. They have nothing to do with us and our behavior as managers or our behavior as a management body. I wash myself clean and the dirt is on the other person. The problem of resistance is taken care of and disposed of. And with it the question of guilt: the other person or persons are the cause, responsible for the resistance, the lack of implementation, or the impending failure (Dent and Goldberg 1999, p. 37; Ford et al. 2008, p. 365). Not me. And finally: the resistance – that's what the others do. They block me, throw sticks, and try to sabotage what has been sensibly planned. They don't behave properly, violate the norms, refuse to comply, try to destroy. In contrast, I dedicate myself to the well-being of the organization, try to save it, keep it functioning, or ensure that it still exists in many years' time.

In the healthcare organization HMO, where the organization was equipped with computers, a manager says – as quoted earlier:

*"I'm tired of dealing with ignorant women who don't appreciate the value of computers."*

The manager vents his anger and makes it clear that the cause of the malaise is to be found in the people's poor character: their lack of interest, their unwillingness to embrace the new, their self-inflicted ignorance. The words also resonate with the accusation that the women addressed are simple-minded and stupid. This is also reflected in the women addressed. This has nothing to do with management and direct leadership from the point of view of the manager speaking. Krantz (1999, p. 42, in Knowles and Linn 2004b, p. 304) formulates this aptly: "At its worst, organizational resistance has been used as a not-so-disguised way of blaming the less powerful for unsatisfactory results of change efforts."

When it comes to the question of guilt, psychologizing or pathologizing can also become an instrument or a weapon used against the other person: when dealing with whistleblowers, we found (see section 2.3) that they were usually fired immediately. If this was not possible, the organization suddenly devalued their work performance to be able to fire them later. If even the claim of incompetence did not stand up to scrutiny, management sometimes resorted to a surprising and frightening tactic: they tried to have the whistleblowers labeled as crazy. To this end, management sent the whistleblowers to an internal or external psychologist and informed the psychologist that they were out of their mind or appeared to be suffering from paranoia. On closer inspection, however, a psychologist found that the individuals were neither crazy nor disturbed by alcohol and drugs, but simply desperate because of the constant harassment by their superiors (Rothschild and Miethe 1994, p. 265).

## Taking Alternative Routes Instead of Shortcuts

Various questions can now be asked: Do people really not feel like it or is the management not oriented toward real needs? Are people afraid or are they just angry that something that directly affects them has been decided over their heads? Are people lazy or have they learned in the organization that they will only get into trouble if they speak up? Is my opponent a sneaky type or is this tactical behavior not a widespread phenomenon in our organization to which I also contribute? Is my colleague hysterical or has she simply become louder because I have failed to listen to her important concerns many times? The picture changes. Suddenly it's no longer just a reaction that shouldn't be taken seriously or a deviant behavior that needs to be sanctioned, but it suddenly has something to do with me. Or it has to do with the leadership relationship or with the organizational culture in which I live and which I also shape.

Managers should not see psychological explanations as a medical or psychotherapeutic assessment or as a useful tool and should certainly not apply them prematurely. Nevertheless, as will become clear in the following Chapter 6, such explanations can clarify statements and behaviors of individuals and in shaping resistance situations. In the following case, it is not possible to apply psychological explanations appropriately. A manager reports on an employee who worked in the laboratory for 20 years and carried out cleaning work there. She had a relatively high salary. Working in the laboratory was also considered more valuable. Then there came a restructuring and, according to the manager, the employee "had to" change departments.

*"She was extremely obstructive, went on sick leave and applied for benefits from the social services. She didn't pass on the knowledge she had accumulated over the years and ignored employees who had to be trained by her. During this time, her husband also died. After a few weeks of mental sick leave, she returned. This was followed by threats of 'no longer seeing any sense in life,' returning to Italy, etc. This employee had built up a small kingdom in the lab and she was the queen. Her loss of status was enormous. Now she had to work in the cleaning service, do shifts on Sundays and public holidays, and had to mingle with the common people. Before, she said she worked in the laboratory when asked about her job. When it came to wages, she was given vested rights. She then did her work as a mediocre employee."*

Psychological explanations such as a perceived loss of status or broken pride seem understandable against the background of the narrative. They explain the employee's resistance to the reorganization. For the employee, this is a major turning point in her professional career, of which she seems to be very proud. Against the background of her previous history, she must feel set back by the reorganization. It seems as if the narrating manager suspects the devastating effect this transfer will have on the employee concerned. Let's assume that this was the case. Then the statement that the decision "had to" be made in this way sounds like a constraint and that no consideration was given to individual sensitivities in the reorganization. The employee was forced and thus became the object or victim of the reorganization. The management thus accepts the negative consequences for the employee. If all this is true, the critical question arises as to whether the decision could not have been made differently, considering the employee's motives, individual sensitivities, and performance.

## 5.2  "One Third Is Always Against It Anyway"

In the various assumptions of the previous section, the causes of resistance are seen in the general characteristics or specific dispositions of people. Several employees then offer resistance and belong to the group of opponents, insurgents, or resisters. Not everyone is resisting, but how many are resisting? How big is the problem? A widely used rule of thumb helps to estimate the quantity problem. A soon-to-be-retired member of the management of a production company in the chemical industry reports that an assessment was carried out for management succession planning. The aim was to find those people from the company's own management team who had sufficient potential for the management team. He describes the employees' reactions as follows:

> *"We formulate requirements and function profiles for all management positions, such as Head of HR or COO. And then we look at the middle management to see who might fit into these different areas. We told them that and then realized … there's this rule … a third were very enthusiastic, a third didn't care and a third were completely opposed. It was always like that. You actually have to take care of those who don't care, because you can still get them on your side."*

The fact that a third are against it is treated as a law of nature that has always applied: it was, is, and always will be the case that people are against it and act in opposition. From this perspective, resistance becomes a completely objective phenomenon that emerges when decisions, changes, or announcements are made by the management and completely independently of what the management does or fails to do. Resistance has nothing to do with what the management does or fails to do, and this pattern also appears again and again in the previous self-understandings.

But there is a second aspect: it is a very clever formula for organizing majorities and minorities. If one third is against it, then two thirds are in favor or don't care; but they are certainly not against it. This is reassuring because you have the (silent) majority on your side or can do something to win over a few more undecided people. This gives you the feeling of having the upper hand and makes you capable of acting. This rule of thirds has the status of a very practical theory, which has become an incontrovertible certainty because it was developed in practice and is recited again and again. It is so clear, so plausible, and is experienced in everyday practice. It is common, if not cultural, knowledge. Who would dare to contradict such a rule, especially as it has long been proven to be correct? The rule thus becomes an effective and powerful rhetorical tool and calms the minds of the management.

If resistance is to be expected anyway, then the chances are 100% that resistance will emerge. Resistance thus becomes a self-fulfilling prophecy in that the behavior and statements of others are interpreted in such a way that the prophecy is confirmed (Dent and Goldberg 1999, p. 38; Ford et al. 2008, p. 263 et seq.). What you expect to find is what you find, which in turn confirms the assumption that resistance is inevitable: one third is always against it anyway, people become more patient as they get older, men drive better than women, the Dutch are stingy, and so on. All of this is completely normal, you don't have to be surprised by it, you should just accept it and, therefore, you don't have to deal with it in terms of content. If it is the case that one third is always against it, then as a manager you have to have a thick skin, be able to put up with it, look past it, or smile it away. Resistance that is experienced as unpleasant is the bullet that a manager has to bite. But since it is a universal rule (i.e. it is the same everywhere and managers everywhere have to bite this bullet), the suffering becomes more bearable. The problem may be annoying, but it is taken care of, or rather, disposed of.

## Taking Alternative Routes Instead of Shortcuts

Constructing resistance as a majority or minority problem inevitably leads to an unproductive politicization of relations. It is no longer about the content of the resistance, about whether it is appropriate and whether new and serious findings are associated with it. If majorities are secured for the decision or the management's assessment, the legitimacy is on the side of the management, and it is sufficiently robust to assert itself against the minority. However, this creates an opposition with clear fronts, and it is only a matter of stabilizing the majority situation

as far as possible. Expressing dissenting opinions quickly lands
you in the camp of the opponents and you are harshly accused
of not being sufficiently loyal. The dissenter's trust is withdrawn,
and it becomes difficult for them to regain it. This form of politicization is unproductive because it is exclusively concerned with
stabilizing power relations, and resistance is stylized as a threat to
these power relationships.

Organizations are always political entities, but the political
game can be played in different ways. I advocate understanding
here. Resistance then becomes an occasion and a sign that such
an understanding is necessary, regardless of how many people are
visibly resisting. Instead of cultivating antagonisms and looking
to secure one's own position of power, the aim should be to initiate an exchange about different perspectives, opinions, interests,
and convictions.

## 5.3 "Where I Am, There Is Reason"

All forms of psychologization and pathologization explain
the phenomenon of resistance. They take care of the problem
of resistance by blaming the other person. The attribution
of deficient characteristics to the person of the resistor also
devalues them. This projects and constructs an image of the
resistor and raises the question of which self-image goes hand
in hand with this. How does the person who is confronted with
the resistance see themselves? In a nutshell, it can be said in
advance that the devaluation of the other person is linked to a
revaluation of oneself.

### "I Can't Believe He Doesn't See It the Way I Do"

Let's return to the case of Regula, Head of Procurement at an
electricity company (see section 2.2) and look again at very

specific statements. Regula reports that there is a high probability that she and other managers at her level will be faced with the centralization of IT at group level. She states the following about her colleague Urs:

*"I can't understand why he doesn't realize what's going to happen here on a large scale."*

The manager expresses her astonishment that the colleague does not recognize this development and does not anticipate it as she does. From her point of view, the development is clear. Her own point of view becomes an unavoidable fact. There is no conceivable argument or justification that could cast doubt on this development and its necessity. Accordingly, the colleague's argumentation can only be irrational (i.e. unreasonable, obsessed with power, and oriented toward the past). Her own point of view is rational. In this case, it would probably be helpful to exchange perspectives, assessments, and reasons in order to get out of the (presumably mutual) negative attribution of irrationality. However, the manager telling the story is and remains stunned that her colleague does not think in the same way or rationally as she does.

In another case, an experienced consultant reports on the implementation of two applications in public administration. The project was 9–12 months behind schedule. He proposed a solution:

*"I was of the opinion that I had found a good solution for everyone involved, both for our company (image, additional costs due to the project delay) and for the customer (employment of its employees and no project delay). As a result, there was practically no project delay and the team was able to continue working."*

He worked out the solution for the customer down to the last detail and prepared the presentation for the customer. He emphasized that the solution had no impact on operations and was an elegant solution for everyone. He was firmly convinced of his proposal and believed that the customer would support it. But things turned out differently from what he had imagined. In the meeting, he realized that his solution was not wanted and that all the disadvantages of the delay were accepted. The customer wanted to stick to the original order:

> *"I can't remember the arguments. At the time, I didn't understand why the customer was against the proposed solution, why there was so much resistance and why I wasn't successful with the solution. At the time, I didn't want to find out whether there were any unnamed reasons for the resistance, as the situation was generally muddled. I was disappointed and didn't understand why the customer decided against it."*

The completely surprising and, from his point of view, irrational reaction does not fit into the context of his reasoning, and he does not know how to deal with it. So, it becomes a frustrating work experience. Only after a longer period of distance from the event is it possible for him to categorize this professional failure differently. He succeeds in doing so by freeing himself from the idea that there is no rationality per se that all people follow, but that all those involved have rationalities and that these can be contradictory. He comes to the realization that the others also have valid, rational reasons and that he did not see them because he was too convinced of his own reasons:

> *"I assume the customer had reasons that were incomprehensible to me or that I perhaps didn't even realize because of my convictions."*

## "Opposition to Our Correct Solution Is Merely Unproductive"

Opposition in this picture is therefore completely surprising, as one's own view is – quite obviously – the correct one. I refer to the previous assumption. The resistance described is then just annoying and energy-wasting. It is particularly disturbing when others do not agree with our "correct expert opinion" in decision-making processes. A manager in the IT sector reports on a meeting to which she and the marketing manager had invited the owner. They wanted to discuss the shift of the marketing budget to online marketing with him within an hour. The online marketing budget was to be increased from CHF 70 000 to CHF 160 000 at the expense of print and radio advertising, while the overall budget of CHF 800 000 was to remain unchanged. Meeting documents were sent out in advance. However, the meeting turned out differently from what they expected:

> *"The owner's questioning led to a very special dynamic in which the marketing manager felt personally attacked. The meeting lasted three and a half hours. A lot of new questions came up that also needed to be clarified. In my view, this also came about because people had not dealt with the topic before the meeting and did not understand social media marketing or the efficient use of a social media platform at all. After the meeting, I asked myself whether the contradictions were constructive or whether they undermined the efficient process and the focus on the objectives."*

The narrator sees himself as an expert in the relevant field, has prepared the meeting well with documents and a clear proposal, and has therefore done everything that needs to be done to take such a decision. According to the narrating manager, the resistance is due to two things: firstly, the inadequate attitude to work (insufficient preparation) and secondly, the resulting lack of understanding of the subject matter. What should have happened from the manager's point of view? The owner should simply have prepared himself properly, then he would have understood and supported the request. The irrational behavior (inadequate preparation) leads to an irrational view of the matter (unnecessary counterarguments) and to an equally irrational course of events (too long, inefficient duration of the meeting). What effect does the resistance have on the manager and the marketing manager? As the resistance is seen as consistently irrational, it is not only directed against the issue, but also against the person. The marketing manager therefore perceives the discussion as a questioning of him as a person and as an expression of personal rejection.

The problem in this narrative seems to be that the narrating manager (and the marketing manager) only attribute rationality to themselves and not to the others. A lot of other questions can be asked that would have allowed the participants to evaluate the meeting and their own work differently: Was our preparation so good that the owner was able to prepare accordingly as we expected? What exactly did we expect? Were these expectations justified, also regarding the duration of the preparation time? Did the owner even have time to prepare? Did we have sufficiently good reasons for our application? Did we listen carefully to the objections, did we take them seriously, did we respond to them? Are the queries not also an expression of a differentiated interest and the desire to understand the matter better and to reach a decision that the owner can also stand by? The resistance shown and felt would then not simply be unproductive, but an important signal for the manager and the head of marketing.

## "I Assert My Version of Reality"

In the previous sections, we encountered managers who are unable to understand when others do not think as they do. The resistance they experience easily reinforces the self-image that their own view is rational and that of others is irrational. In the following case, a manager of an accounts department in the automotive industry describes how he deals with irrational resistance. He argues that it happens everywhere and is therefore completely normal for employees and colleagues to be required to comply with processes and fill out forms. He notes with slight amusement:

> *"It's hard to believe how creative some people get when it comes to finding reasons why they don't have to fill out these forms. It feels like it takes more time to find these creative ways than to fill out the forms, but for some employees it's worth the detours. The main thing is to put up resistance."*

The unreasonable resistance is directed against the reasonable demand to fulfill the duty. From the narrator's point of view, the requirements are justified, necessary, and correct in their current form. Any doubt is therefore neither appropriate nor understandable. However, the resistance cannot be averted, it comes automatically and must be met with steadfastness and intransigence. Resistance is pushed aside, and this is precisely what stabilizes and confirms the manager's self-image.

> *"Resistance can therefore be overcome. A certain persistence helps. If you remain consistent, you will initially be met with skepticism. Sure, the other person won't achieve their goal. Over time, the skepticism then turns into a kind of respect or even admiration for having withstood the resistance."*

The manager is the rock in the sea. He is the hero who stands his ground against all resistance and asserts himself out of the unwavering conviction that he is right. He stands by what he has decided and implements it in the face of resistance. With this self-image, learning and development mean that the others give up their resistance and adapt to what the manager has defined as the correct and necessary guidelines and to which they have irrevocably adhered:

*"After a while, people realize that it is easier to stick to the guidelines and that they have a right to exist. They may even have advantages. Eyes are opened."*

By devaluing resistance as irrational and unjustified, the annoying duty to resist it remains, but there is no need to deal with it in terms of content. Insisting on your own reality closes your eyes to other possible good reasons. In this case, it is about enforcing the rule. However, the attitude could just as well be adopted that rules and guidelines are designed based on joint developments and ongoing feedback in such a way that they are well understood, easy to follow, and efficient to fulfill and can be abolished or further developed in the event of new findings. In this way, realities would be continually reinvented instead of having to constantly assert rationality against the irrationality of others.

## Taking Alternative Routes Instead of Shortcuts

This touches on a very fundamental point in the common understanding of managers. Managers usually associate management with the idea of being firm and steadfast. The superior should not follow the others. Taking a stand is important so that others know where they stand and the manager is predictable (Müller and Endrissat 2006, p. 10). The manager must show his colors, be straightforward, and not hide behind flimsy justifications, other people, or the decisions of others. It is precisely this view that is expressed in the stories. The managers represent their view of things and do not allow themselves to be dissuaded despite resistance. But this firmness can also mean becoming rigid and immovable. Holding on to one's own position does not mean taking note of the other point of view or the arguments of others. By identifying the other side as the source of resistance and judging and devaluing the articulation of contradiction as unreasonable, it is impossible to weigh up different points of view. In this way, steadfastness becomes an unyielding adherence to one's own position and point of view, with the result that the other person's concerns and perspectives are not taken seriously. Instead of retreating to one's own position, insisting on it and viewing resistance as disruptive or simply smiling at it, the management should also be willing to engage with other points of view to arrive at a prudent and balanced judgment and then stand firm in defending it.

## 5.4 "Thinking at the Top, Doing at the Bottom"

The hierarchy of an organization has a specific task or function. It has to ensure, review, integrate, and meaningfully develop the organizational performance or ensure all of this. Organizations differ greatly in the specific form of the hierarchy; for example, it can be flat or steep, influence can be concentrated at the top or widely distributed throughout the organization, or the hierarchy can strengthen or undermine individual responsibility. There are therefore many ways of structuring the hierarchy in the organization, and what is ultimately considered appropriate or suitable depends largely on the self-image of the actors involved.

### "Management Controls the Lower Level"

From the assumption that management controls the lower levels, it is sometimes inferred that management alone is responsible for carrying out the complex strategic thinking, looking ahead and correctly interpreting market signals. They and they alone are responsible for these demanding tasks because, after all, management holds the relevant position, is expected to do so, and is paid appropriately for it. It is precisely for this reason that career advancement also tests whether a person has conceptual and strategic skills. Logically, this means that the most capable and strategically minded people are at the top of the company. Top management, and only top management, is responsible for adapting the organization to the market and the environment (e.g. Eisenhardt et al. 2010). So *is* top management the organization? No, it is not. Even if top managers are influential, this view obscures the view of what makes up organizations and largely change: employees, relationships, perspectives, networks, habits, processes, dogmas, superstitions, etc. However, the seeds of resistance are already sown when one group of people claims the privilege of being above all other assessments of the situation (Cunha et al. 2013) and sees itself alone as authorized and capable of recognizing the future and reconfiguring the organization according to its own ideas.

## "Management Makes the Plan"

Let us recall the department secretary's report on the merger of three organizational units in section 2.2, which were then to be placed under one management. This resulted in a never-ending resistance and a grueling power struggle that lasted for years, in which many people fell by the wayside. For the top managers, it was a matter of course that they alone had to design the far-reaching reorganization, and they also found this a motivating and fulfilling activity. A fun task that then led to a clean, appealing result: this is what the new building of the future should look like, now it just had to be built. However, the fact that those affected by the decision had a completely different view of the reorganization and might not be equally enthusiastic was lost sight of. Their own enthusiasm for their own plan blinded them:

*"It's super interesting when you can operate with such organizations in the green field, so to speak. We mainly thought about the fields of activity and the organizations, which have to function efficiently. We never thought about the people, or rarely did."*

## "Employees Must Carry Out Instructions"

The organization mutates into an instrument in the hands of top management. What is left for the employees, those at the bottom? They are condemned to a passive, insensitive, and indifferent role. They are expected to carry out what has been dictated to them from above. They agree and (only) have to think about how the vision and the measures can be realized. "Those up there think and those down there do what those up there have come up with." They have to follow instructions and do not have to question the correctness and effectiveness of management decisions. The statement by the marketing director in the bank, in which the branch managers resisted what they saw as a one-sided assessment of marketing, is a good illustration of this view (see section 2.1). See the relevant excerpt from the marketing director's statement:

> *"This is not a thing we are used to, people challenging something that is not contestable. (…) It was incredible that their demands received such an inviting response. (…) And the boss said the new rules were to help the company better oversee the local business units, better control the business. (….) But it was all about consolidating the power of these branch types."*

The idea that a subordinate level of the hierarchy takes a stand against top management is an outrageous act, an aberration, a dereliction of duty. It turns hierarchical logic on its head, because suddenly those at the bottom start thinking instead of accepting and implementing the management's decision. Autonomy is honorable, but it certainly shouldn't go that far, because management takes care of the big picture and employees should take care of their specific work and do it independently. The mental work of management simply must not be competed with; otherwise – in this idea – the order of the organization will be turned completely upside down. And if order is called into question, chaos threatens, and the organization loses its efficiency.

In this understanding, employees do not have the right to challenge management with other positions. "Where would that get us?" The marketing manager had expected the boss to act and order compliance with the top management's decision. From his point of view, his job would have been to restore order.

## Taking Alternative Routes Instead of Shortcuts

Don't we live in a world today in which employers are particularly attractive when employees can and should be actively involved in decisions that affect their area of work, but also the organization as a whole, or when people outside the organization are integrated into innovation and development processes via open innovation itself? In the case of the bank (see section 2.1), the position of marketing director does not gain the upper hand; top management allows middle managers to temporarily enter the top management's sphere of influence and responsibility. However, there are also organizations in which there are generally clear boundaries that must not be crossed. And if these boundaries are crossed after all, the deviators are subject to sanctions. Whilst thinking outside the box is desirable, it is only outside of what management has decided or what management assumes should be implemented because it is the right thing to do. Change processes can lead to areas of influence and responsibility that were previously defined as independent being overridden by a management decision.

There are decisions in which employees can understand that they do not participate. However, there are just as many areas in which it would be expedient, sensible, and motivating to think along with. In this way, the factual and cultural knowledge available in the organization can be used comprehensively to make more prudent decisions. "But we can't always involve everyone," is often the response. Of course not. This is neither necessary nor (usually) expected. The task of management is to assess when this is necessary and sensible and how such involvement can take place. This creates new management tasks: the meaningfulness of involvement must be assessed, the involvement must then be properly organized, and the decision must then be made on the basis of a wide range of information, which may well be contradictory and ambiguous, and justified in the organization in a convincing and comprehensible manner. The aim is not to create an organization without resistance, as resistance often only becomes visible in the participation process. Rather, the aim is to avoid unnecessary resistance. And it is unnecessary when it is foreseeable; for example, when decisions are made over people's heads, their knowledge and experience are not recognized, or their professional identity is not respected. A prudent management process design avoids this unnecessary resistance and understands resistance as an integral part of the organization with which a serious debate takes place. In this way, the order of the organization is not destroyed; rather, it is an alternative idea of what "good order" is.

## 5.5 "Management Must Fight the Inertia of the Organization"

Resistance to change is often explained on the one hand by an innate human inertia, as we saw in section 5.1. On the other hand, it is also assumed that the organization has a natural tendency toward inertia (Cunha et al. 2013). Management is responsible for developing plans and ensuring that these plans are put into practice. If only it weren't for the resistance that can thwart all management efforts! This is how BP (British Petroleum) justified the oil spill in the Gulf of Mexico and the fact that it could not be sufficiently contained. BP intended to transform itself into bp (Beyond Petroleum) and thus into a sustainable and green company pursuant to a management decision. All efforts to create a clean image were destroyed at a stroke when the Deepwater Horizon oil platform triggered one of the worst environmental disasters on 20 April 2010, and an estimated 800 million liters of oil leaked from a well in the Gulf of Mexico over a period of almost three months. As reported in February 2013, the US government planned to present extensive evidence of willful and negligent conduct by the company. The US government's lawyer, Michael Underhill, said that the main blame lay with BP. A "culture of neglecting safety" had prevailed within the company. Out of greed for profit, "reckless behavior" was tolerated and sometimes even encouraged. BP, as the owner of the platform, admitted that it had made mistakes, but accused the operating company Transocean of failing to maintain the facility properly. The subcontractor Halliburton is also alleged to have used inferior materials, which led to the uncontrolled leakage of oil and the explosion and fire on the rig. The company denied responsibility for poor management by blaming others. The company was not responsible for the disaster. BP did indeed take its responsibility seriously, but – and this was BP's point – the subcontractors resisted by not implementing the sound management system designed by BP (Cunha et al. 2013). The rationale for resisting implementation was to avoid or at least reduce costly fines. This is a widespread idea: change (in this case the transition to a sustainable company) inevitably produces resistance (in this case the noncompliance with the requirements of the sustainable company), and management is required to overcome this resistance (Dent and Goldberg 1999, p. 25).

## "The Organization Is Fundamentally Lazy"

What applies to individuals also applies to organizations. The entire organization is said to have rigid patterns that resist change. It takes an effort on the part of management to act against the inertia of the organization and overcome it. In some cases, the idea is that structures or processes need to be broken up to dissolve the bunker mentality or backyard thinking. For example, one bank manager reported that his area of responsibility was geared toward providing a "service to the customer." After his bank was acquired by another, he was repeatedly told by employees and customers during the integration process that various processes were no longer efficient and customer friendly. Due to his management responsibility, his long-standing customer relationship, and his back-office experience, he tried to achieve an improvement within the large bank with the groups involved in the process. Initially, all parties agreed on the need for change. Over time, however, the bank manager had to realize:

> *"In the end, people hid behind 'pretexts' that were not tangible. Nobody wanted to expose themselves or take a risk. It is now clear to me that large service providers (in the financial world, for example) will 'only' be able to offer customers a few modular, standardized products and services in the future due to increasing regulation. It therefore comes as no surprise to me that the majority of employees in these companies have a culture of fear or 'service by the book.' I get the same picture from large companies in the insurance, food, and transportation sectors. As this type of service provision did not match my expectations, I resigned."*

On the one hand, the manager explains the unfortunate failure of the change project he himself initiated in psychological terms. He concludes that the members of the organization no longer wanted to take risks, for example. However, the manager does not explain the behavior in terms of the person's characteristics, but rather attributes it to cultural developments in many large companies. The bank's culture produces certain behaviors that cannot be overcome, and this was reflected in the subtle resistance to the change he led. The manager explains the resistant behavior in terms of organizational sociology: according to his analysis, the resistance to deviating from rules that provide security is rooted in the culture of the organization. The organization, like many other organizations, had become inert and had trained the people working there to behave inertly. The narrating manager has a self-image (I am courageous, take risks, expose myself, am consistent) that does not match the culture of the company he is analyzing and, in line with his self-image, draws the consequences. However, it can be argued that there may be completely different explanations for the behavior or this perception, which have nothing to do with the inertia of the organization, but rather, for example, with the role that the manager held or was assigned, or with an unproductive project dynamic. However, the manager here is resorting to a very general and widespread explanation of organizational inertia that does not necessarily do justice to the specific situation. If a hasty psychological explanation is referred to as psychologizing, this explanation can be described as "sociologizing."

## "You Have to Shake Things Up, Exert Pressure, and Sometimes Use Coercion"

The idea of an inherent inertia in people and organizations has consequences: without stimulation, without a shake-up, people settle in comfortably, even sink into lethargy. Organizations turn to stone. If they can afford it, they simply perform poorly or perish. It is made clear to employees that they now have to get out of their comfort zone or be taken out of it. However, such statements by management are read as insinuations. As a result, management loses its legitimacy, especially if management is perceived as distant and it is assumed that it has little idea of how (stressful) the everyday lives of employees or middle managers are.

According to this view, managers have to keep pushing, otherwise the system stops, rusts, calcifies, and is not viable. The organization is like a billiard ball at rest that has to be knocked by the white ball, the management, in order for it to move (i.e. for changes to take place at all). However, this movement is finite. A perpetual motion machine is unthinkable. The management must therefore keep nudging, kicking it on. Management is therefore forced to impose changes against the resistance (inertia) of the organization or parts of the organization. This also legitimizes the fact that the members of the organization are not involved in change projects, as they would do anything to resist the changes anyway.

## Taking Alternative Routes Instead of Shortcuts

In the understanding outlined above, consistency and stability are reinterpreted as negative inertia, as an old burden. It could also be that clinging to the existing is a justified expression of criticism of the new, which does not suit the management. The hasty conclusion is that the past, the existing routines, are devalued across the board. They may be functional or a particular strength or even the pride of the employees. The either-or game "Are you for the future or are you a diehard?" only poses the question of loyalty but is not a differentiated and appreciative way of dealing with the status quo. Furthermore, it is also known

(Nagel 2001) that it takes time to leave existing routines or cultural patterns behind or to understand what makes a management or leadership relationship, a group, or an organization tick in the first place. The mere request to leave something behind, the devaluation of what is already there or even the threat of sanctions for non-compliance are counterproductive. By contrast, the value of consistency should be recognized to preserve the experiences, investments, and loyalties acquired in the past and use them for the future (De Wit and Meyer 2004, p. 170).

Finally, it is now also known that the inertia of organizations is overestimated, and the importance of continuous, ongoing change is underestimated, as managers either take too little notice of it or do not allow it at all. The renowned organizational researcher Weick (2000, p. 237) states:

> *"We are enthralled by the story of dramatic interventions in which heroic figures turn around stubbornly inertial structures held in place by rigid people who are slow learners."*

If management pays more attention to the changes that are constantly occurring and promotes them, it has to initiate planned change processes much less frequently and can do so in a more targeted manner. An important part of organizational change occurs continuously and emanates from all levels of the organization as people make minor and major changes in their work. They proceed according to the principle of trial and error, make mistakes and experience successes, and the findings then spread to other parts of the organization (Kerber and Buono 2005, p. 27).

## 5.6 Reflecting Instead of Taking Shortcuts

The hasty conclusions in this chapter show that resistance is the annoying coffee stain on an otherwise beautifully white tablecloth.

Resistance disrupts, inhibits, and stands in the way of shaping sustainable organizations. It must be accepted, can be overlooked, or must be cleared out of the way. Resistance has a consistently negative connotation in these guiding principles. But something else also stands out. Jumping to conclusions (Kahneman 2011) does a service to those who draw and express them. However, if the aim is to deal productively with resistance, they do us a disservice:

- **Normalization and reassurance:** Resistance loses its drama because it is completely normal, and because it is normal, there is no need to deal with it.

- **Security:** Since we argue rationally and the resistors are irrational and we are in a working world in which only rational justifications are valid, we are in the right.

- **Justification:** For the organization to be developed, we have to decide the direction and, if necessary, enforce it with coercion. The organization and the people living in it would not move of their own accord anyway.

- **Sovereignty:** Resistors are in the minority in any case, so they have no political weight and their concerns do not have to be taken seriously.

- **Delegating away the question of guilt:** Resistance is caused by the person offering resistance or by the culture of the organization and has nothing to do with me or my management or leadership behavior. We are off the hook.

This would be another good time to make fun of the management, to accuse them of incompetence or a lack of insight. It would be a very common stylistic device. It is easy to denigrate practitioners and managers as uninformed, stupid, and dull-witted. You could write a book with the title *Healthy Reactions to Bad Management? Is There Anything Left to Save?* Just as nowadays

bankers are often accused of being greedy across the board or as
Günter Ogger slandered German managers as failures, wasters,
jailbirds, quacks, bores, and the like in his 1992 book *Nieten in
Nadelstreifen* (Duffers in Pinstripes). Such sweeping generaliza-
tions and polemics are always entertaining and, as Ogger's book
shows, they promise high sales figures. But demonstratively displayed malice and accusations get us nowhere. In essence, they
are nothing more than hasty, populist, and unfounded prejudices
designed to attract attention. The result would be a flood of
mutual accusations: the forward-pushing management against
the obstructive, unruly employees or the clever employees against
the obtuse managers. The members of the organization are
divided and there are clear fronts. This would lead to a dubious
and unproductive, albeit ironically entertaining, game of "black and
white" and would only fuel the rivalry between management
and employees that has been conjured up time and again.

Let's get back to the point of why managers make use of the
assumptions and explanations presented in this chapter, which
are not written in any management textbook and are not taught
in any serious educational institution. Such guiding principles are
passed on informally and are considered so fundamental that they
do not even need to be taught. They are there, they apply, and
you can use them at appropriate moments and then make sense
of things. As final explanations, they enable us to be in control
of the situation, as we quickly understand or see through what is
happening before our eyes. And they help us to feel competent
and confident in our everyday (management or leadership) work.
Nevertheless, there are conclusions that we draw, explanations
that we have in our repertoire that can be classified as premature.
We automatically apply them because we assume that they are
valid. After all, they are confirmed time and time again or they
have helped us to remain in control of the situation. They give
us security and a sense of competence in the performance of

our profession and function. The explanations fly to us, so to speak; we don't even have to think about them for long. They are always available and because they are so concise, everything becomes clear immediately. But the speed with which generally precise observations can be explained is not in itself a guarantee of quality. Rather, it is a potential trap that can snap shut and narrow our view. If we apply explanations automatically, we have no opportunity to think them through in terms of their underlying assumptions. In doing so, we deprive ourselves of the opportunity to see events differently, to question ourselves and to choose other paths.

The aim of this chapter is to encourage such reflection, particularly at those points in the chapter where you feel personally addressed, where you recognize yourself or others.

## Summary

- Every person has certain assumptions about others, themselves, and how they should behave in specific situations that they take for granted. In situations of resistance, these specific, unquestioned assumptions are applied and take effect.

- Some assumptions are shortcuts or hasty conclusions that lead to unproductive results and thus to a dead end.

- The hasty conclusions are based on stereotypical ideas about people, about the causes of resistance, about majority or minority relationships in the organization, about oneself, about who is allowed to control and influence the organization, and about the nature of the organization.

- However, jumping to conclusions also brings (questionable) benefits because it makes it possible, for example, to transfer responsibility for difficulties or failure to others and to justify one's own unreflective behavior.

# 6

# What Is Behind Resistance: Explanatory Models

If you want to know rightly, you must first have doubted rightly.

—Aristotle

In the previous chapters, I presented concrete stories and case studies of resistance and reflected on the specific situations. Many examples were used to illustrate how resistance can manifest and express itself and how dealing with resistance is sometimes more and other times less successful. Furthermore, the aim was to identify assumptions that repeatedly appear in stories told by managers, which are memorable and common, but at the same time abbreviated. Although we are awake in everyday life, management and leadership practically sleepwalk through everyday life and therefore also encounter situations in which we identify resistance. So not everything happens "in the brightness

151

of consciousness" (Neuberger 1995, p. 298). This means that the significance of such assumptions and their consequences are not simply obvious. For this reason, they were examined and discussed in more detail.

This chapter contains explanatory models that claim to provide in-depth insights into the origins of resistance and the dynamics of resistance processes. The requirement for these scientifically sound explanatory models is that they make explicit which assumptions they are based on and justify these assumptions. The explanatory model must ultimately stand up to critical scrutiny. By contrast, the self-evident assumptions presented in Chapter 5 are generally considered to be proven, correct, and valid, even without scientific scrutiny. Under normal circumstances, there is no need to examine them critically (Nagel and Holzer 2012, p. 20). However, as we saw in the previous chapter, it is worth taking a critical look at these self-evident assumptions. As we will see in this chapter, however, individual scientific explanatory models do not stand up to critical scrutiny either.

The insights to be gained in this chapter will never be able to explain everything that has to do with resistance. And let us not kid ourselves: knowing more does not necessarily mean understanding everything better, but it also means acknowledging that we do not understand something. On the contrary, gaining more knowledge reveals more clearly what we do not know. Leadership researcher Keith Grint (2010, p. 1 et seq.) reflects on this in a sympathetic way:

> *"When I began reading leadership literature in about 1986, I had already spent some time in various leadership positions, so at that time I'd read little, but I understood everything about the subject from the University of Life. Then, as I read more material, I realized that all my previous 'truths' were built on very dubious foundations, so my understanding decreased as my knowledge increased. 2006 was a difficult year: I'd read hundreds, if not thousands of books and articles,*

*and concluded that Socrates was right – wisdom only comes when you realize how ignorant you are. I think I'm now on the road to recovery and have gotten past base camp (...)."*

This self-irony is good because the loss of certainty is certainly not pleasant. But by gaining insight, not only are certainties lost, but it becomes clear that there are no compelling necessities, but at most alternatives that have to be weighed up against each other. This creates options for action.

This chapter is structured as follows: first, it deals with explanations that start with the individual person (section 6.1). Then the relationship between the actors involved in resistance situations is examined (section 6.2). And finally, the organizational level takes center stage (section 6.3 and section 6.4). References are repeatedly made to previous chapters.

# 6.1 Resistance from the Perspective of Psychology

## Outdated Approaches of Psychologizing Psychology

One of the criticisms made in the previous chapters was that the causes and origins of resistance are seen in the person. In addition to personalization, I criticized the fact that the resisters were generally assigned specific, mostly negative characteristics that were supposed to justify the resistance (psychologization) or the people were described as crazy or sick in one way or another (pathologization). If we now look at the findings of psychological research, it should be noted that this section is only concerned with whether and, if so, how resistance in organizations is modeled and explained from this perspective.

Older psychological approaches assume that resistance is a stable characteristic of the person and thus a potential reaction to change (Knowles and Linn 2004a, p. 6). When it comes to resistant reactions to change, these classic and now also heavily criticized psychological approaches distinguish between behaviors that generally adapt to change (adaptive) and those that are considered poorly adapted (maladaptive). For example, a humorous comment on a change project is considered adaptive and a refusal is considered maladaptive (Bovey and Hede 2000). In this way, resistance quickly becomes a reactive act of disobedience, whereby the decisive factor is to what extent this behavior can be classified as disobedient. If the person in question only behaves a little disobediently, it cannot be assumed that they are really resisting. If, on the other hand, a person rebels loudly, they will not conform but will resist and cause problems in changing projects. It is therefore concluded that this behavior is detrimental to the organization and is therefore described as maladaptive. Certain behaviors are assessed as resistance. They are characterized as maladaptive behavior and thus judged as negative without restriction. In this line of research, the actors therefore resist inappropriately, which means that their resistance is a priori considered illegitimate (Jermier et al. 1994, p. 6). Resistance is thus clearly evaluated negatively and must be made to disappear. We have already encountered this assumption in Chapter 5. The problem is that resistance is judged negatively by employees without restriction and regardless of the specific context. Without explicitly stating it, the idea can be derived from this that the individual must follow the orders of management.

This research approach completely ignores the perspective of those who offer resistance and ignores the fact that their motives and intentions may be justified and appropriate. For example, various studies show that employees try to focus attention on issues that they believe need to be addressed for the organization to maintain its performance or social legitimacy. By speaking up or complaining, people are taking a risk and are also aware of the risk to a certain extent (Piderit 2000, p. 784 et seq.). This line of research ignores some essential perspectives and implicitly makes questionable value judgments that are neither explained nor justified. Without addressing or problematizing this, it adopts the perspective of management and implicitly justifies the power of management over organizational members as well as sanctions if the duty of obedience is not observed.

Other, equally older psychological approaches assume that people go through a reactive process when they are personally confronted with major change processes. It is assumed that they go through four (or more) phases: initial rejection, resistance, gradual exploration of the changes, and finally acceptance of the changes. One assumption is that change is always perceived as a threat and triggers fears, so that defense mechanisms are activated, which in turn block people's ability to adapt to the changes. Resistance thus becomes a completely natural side effect of change, and people have different abilities and willingness to adapt to change requirements (Bovey and Hede 2000, p. 534).

Criticism of these assumptions is manifold: it is doubtful that such clear reaction patterns always proceed in the same way and in a linear fashion. Nevertheless, such explanatory models are used again and again, presumably because they organize the complex world of management and leadership so nicely. As previously discussed, it is highly questionable that only these (negative) emotions ever arise, and that they always occur in the same order, that change "always" produces resistance and, finally, that resistance should be inherent in the person. It turns out that attitudes to change do not develop according to a typical pattern. Moreover, if negative reactions to change subside over time, this is by no means an expression of approval.

On closer inspection, the assumptions of these psychologizing psychological explanatory models are not convincing and invite premature conclusions. As was shown in various examples in

Chapter 5, but as more recent studies (e.g. Symon 2005) also point out, both psychologization and pathologization serve those who make use of both mechanisms. Psychologization and pathologization deprive the other party of legitimacy and they no longer have to be taken seriously. Then it is not a matter of psychological findings. Psychologizing and pathologizing are simply a means in the internal power struggle. But it is far from the truth to assume that only management uses this "strategic rhetoric." Employees also use it (Symon 2005), as both sides strive to deprive their opponents of the basis for their arguments, to undermine their arguments and to reduce them to absurdity.

## The Ambivalence Between Resistance and Compliance

The attitudes of employees toward change can be captured in three dimensions, each of which relates to one issue: firstly, the dimension of the mind, i.e. the opinion or conviction (cognitive) – "I (do not) believe it"; secondly, the feeling or state of mind (emotional) – "I (do not) like it"; and thirdly, the behavior (intentional) – "I (will not/will) do it" (Knowles and Linn 2004a, p. 5). A common, outdated conclusion is that resistance is due to a negative expression of all three dimensions: "I am against it" (cognitive), "It annoys me" (emotional), "I openly oppose it" (intentional). By contrast, support or approval would automatically be attributed to a positive characteristic: "I think the decision is right," "I am looking forward to the new situation," "I am doing everything I can to make it a success." However, this conclusion proves to be too simple.

For example, people are often ambivalent, undecided, or conflicted about change. This means that the three dimensions do not have to be consistently positive or consistently negative, but individual dimensions can have both positive and negative elements, and positive and negative characteristics can also occur between the dimensions. In addition, this can change again over the course of time. Here are four examples (Piderit 2000, p. 787 et seq.):

1. One employee is convinced that the upcoming change is essential for securing the organization's existence, but at the same time is of the opinion that the approach has not been sufficiently thought through (cognitive).

2. An employee plans to write an anonymous critical article in an external blog but supports the management decision in everyday organizational life out of uncertainty as to how management would react to open criticism (intentional).

3. An employee learns that he no longer has a budget to offer incentives to his salesmen. As the budget cut comes late in the planning cycle, this announcement shocks and frustrates him (emotionally). At the same time, he also welcomes the change, as the budget for product improvements has been increased simultaneously and he is convinced that the salesmen will be able to offer their customers more attractive products as a result (cognitive).

4. A middle manager initially reacts positively to a restructuring and centralization of his organization with the help of the company-wide introduction of new software. He is euphoric (emotional) because he believes that the change is ultimately necessary (cognitive). Over time, his attitude changes as he concludes that management does not provide sufficient support (cognitive). Although he is still convinced that the change is necessary (cognitive), he later speaks out against the dangers of "this mammoth project" (intentional). He is also discouraged by the lack of commitment from his work colleagues (emotional).

It can generally be assumed that most employees react ambivalently to changes or decisions (Piderit 2000, p. 788 et seq.). At this point at the latest, it should become clear how schematic and undifferentiated premature conclusions (e.g. "One third is always against") are. They do not allow us to understand the differentiated arguments. It is no longer possible to quickly draw clear and simple conclusions about individual attitudes from observed behavior. For example: he is upset, he will be against it, or she reacts euphorically, she is fully behind the initiative. If the management investigates the attitudes more closely and comes across such ambivalences, it forms a more accurate picture and does not fall so easily into the political judgment of "they are for and they are against." Exploring (ambivalent) attitudes in more detail may bring some new insights to light and thus make motivations, moods, justifications, and past experiences easier to understand.

## 6.2 Resistance Arising Between People

Let us move away from explanatory models that focus on the individual person and focus on what happens between people. Resistance then arises in or because of relationships and because of the way in which those involved in the relationship shape this relationship. When we talk about relationships, the term is not based on a value judgment. It can therefore refer to both good and bad relationships. It is like the statement by Watzlawick et al. (2011) about communication: "You cannot *not* communicate." Following on from this, we can say: "You cannot *not* have relationships." So even if colleagues are annoyed with each other or no longer want to have anything to do with each other, they still have a relationship that can be qualified as distant and possibly mutually degrading.

Resistance arises due to the way in which the actors involved behave toward and perceive each other. As we have already seen in the previous chapters, it is crucial whether managers interpret resistance as a behavior that is only caused by others, by the employee's fear, by the colleague's desire for power, or by the superior's insecurity about losing status. If, on the other hand, resistance is attributed to the mutual relationship, the causes are no longer so clearly defined.

Let us return to the example of the department secretary (see section 2.2), who pushed for the merger of three organizational units under a single management. At the beginning, he sees resistance from politicians, other managers, and the many employees. Only after many years of seemingly endless power struggles does he establish a connection between the behavior identified as resistance and the behavior of the management body. Only then are simple psychologizations dropped. Only then does it become a relationship story in which all those involved influence each other and in which casualties are no longer clearly distributed. Only then do terms such as "injury" emerge that point to a relationship problem, because an injury is felt by one side of the relationship and inflicted by another side of the relationship.

## Resistance as an Expression of a Damaged Relationship

Even in the early days of dealing with resistance in research, it was recognized that what happens between people (i.e. how relationships are shaped or changed and how this in turn affects the person(s)) must be considered. For example, Coch and French (1948) pointed out early on that change processes that involve employees in their development lead to significantly less resistance than if they are not involved. A little later, Lawrence (1954) showed that resistance can be understood in terms of the loss of social status and the lack of recognition of skills. A person who is demoted due to a change against their will and without being asked is likely to feel unrecognized as a person and as a worker, perceive the measure as a personal degradation, and may even feel humiliated. In this understanding, resistance is an obvious result of how the process is designed by the superior and how the person concerned then perceives this accordingly. However, the responsibility for the resistance perceived by the manager lies with the manager and not with the employee.

Where the damage to the relationship comes from, how it manifests itself, and what it leads to can be extremely varied. Let us look at this using an example. A sales manager in the metal industry vividly describes an episode with the "big boss" at the time, the managing director of the company:

*"So, let's just go to the staff meeting! It was not with great enthusiasm that the employees walked down the corridor in front of me towards the large meeting room. Once again, it was time to listen to our big boss. It finally got quiet and Urs cleared his throat. He just wanted to make sure everyone was listening to him. He began by welcoming us and explaining how the information was to be presented. As I had only been with the company for two months as the sales manager, I watched closely. It was always a question of authority. And what better occasion was there to observe this than at an employee briefing? I listened intently to his sometimes almost chummy statements. Everything was relaxed. He then told us how badly the company was doing. Not a word of this had been mentioned at my interview. So, I also had to hear that no pay rise was possible. I then looked at the faces of the employees and expected to be more disappointed but couldn't really find any. Anyway, the event was somehow wrapped up and it was off to a small aperitif. Everyone enjoyed a beer or snack and discussed everyday problems at work. I somehow didn't quite understand the world after Urs's words. Everyone went home and they all came back the next day. Hardly a word about the information event. Exactly one week later, the boss came to work as usual in the*

*morning. His parking space was right next to his office. After all, he is the boss! But what was he driving up in? A brand new Maserati! Now the employee information became a conversation! Hadn't he said that the company was in a bad way and a pay rise wasn't possible? Now his words, which nobody was interested in earlier, were put on the gold scale! Also in my opinion: nothing but a contradiction!"*

The management relationship between the company boss and the employees is described as intact, personal, and close. The sales manager experienced a surprise during the presentation, as he only now received information that he would have expected during the interview. Was the line manager sincere, had he informed him honestly about the company situation so that he knew what he was getting into? The sales manager may have doubts about the manager's sincerity and may not really know whether he can trust him. Even if the communicated measures brought disadvantages for the employees, they seemed to accept the managing director's reasons. They seemed credible. The manager's message was: "We all have to tighten our belts." "All of us" and not just "you." But when he then drives up in the Maserati, the message changes: "Only you" have to tighten your belts, "I do not." The relationship of trust is damaged. It can be assumed that the employees feel deceived or even lied to. They were led to believe that there was solidarity, but the managing director enjoys all the benefits, does not have to accept any cutbacks, or possibly even gains a personal advantage from the efficiency measures. The sense of justice has been violated. Everything that was previously accepted is now being called into question because the credibility and honesty of the boss is being questioned.

Relationships can be shaped in such a way that they can be described as intact, productive, or workable. However, relationships can also be damaged, which can lead to resistance. To explore and better understand this, resistance events can be interpreted from the perspective of relationship themes and areas of tension. Here are three examples:

- **Devaluation (instead of appreciation):** The hasty conclusions described in Chapter 5 are consistently subject to a devaluation of the resistant person or group of people. They are described as backward, sluggish, anxious, irrational, or even crazy, becoming low-ranking members of the organization who simply have to do what they are told.

- **Artificiality (instead of authenticity):** In the case of the lottery company (see section 3.1), where the sexual harassment awareness workshops are held, the management's approach is perceived as artificial. The humor, as well as the workshop format, the joint development, are intended to conceal the actual concern, the enforcement of the moral-legalistic view.

- **Rejection (instead of acceptance):** Resistance can be experienced as personal rejection (see section 3.5), which deprives the person concerned of legitimacy (as a manager or as a valuable employee).

Other relationship issues such as trust, respect, and belonging are – not only, but also – important in the context of resistance. The following sections take a closer look at the tension between power and powerlessness in its various manifestations.

## Resistance to Attempts to Control

It does not matter what contexts we are in; all relationships are power relationships. Even if your child is supposed to leave the house at 7:40 in the morning and refuses to put on a hat at 7:38, screaming at the top of their voice and unwilling to compromise.

It is extremely cold outside and parental duty of care dictates that they should protect themselves against the cold.[1]

Power plays an important role everywhere, be it between equals or in the hierarchy. Power can be distributed symmetrically or asymmetrically. Neither one nor the other is simply good or bad. If management or leadership relationships are symmetrical, the manager may not be able to fulfill his role properly. If the relationship between formally equal colleagues is asymmetrical, the problem may arise that one person is always subordinate to the other or feels dominated. Or if there is a constant tussle between equals as to who has the upper hand. In management or leadership relationships, we usually accept an asymmetrical relationship if this order of relationships is functional and is seen as fair and just. The hierarchy is considered justified if it handles the rights of control it has been granted with care. There are limits to asymmetrical influence (i.e. when one person can cause another to do something that this person would not otherwise do) (Staehle 1991, p. 372). But where exactly is this limit?

In the previous chapters, we have heard stories in which impressions such as the following have arisen. Decisions were made over the heads of other people or they were presented with a fait accompli. It was expected that the other person would simply accept the decisions or adopt the decision-makers' convictions (over time). In some cases, the resistance ebbs away at some point, is no longer visible, and does not lead to any change in the situation. In other cases, the management tries to push through an issue against the organization, but the resistance puts a spanner in the works. For example, a marketing manager from a retail company explains that a project was launched by top management to generate higher margins from the individual product areas. Consultants from a large, well-known management consultancy

---

[1] Unfortunately, the author is not only familiar with this situation from other people's case histories.

were brought in to support the project. However, the very fact that external consultants from this company were to examine "his" merchandise business caused the marketing manager and the other managers an "inner resistance," which then manifested itself as follows:

> *"During the clarification phase, I only tried to defend and justify my product business. Instead of cooperating with the consultants, I tried to make life difficult for them. During the development of measures, they also met with resistance from me again. Wherever possible, I tried to torpedo the proposed measures as not being expedient."*

The management nevertheless approved some of the measures and the marketing manager then had to implement them with his team. But then the marketing manager himself experienced resistance from his own team, which did not approve of these measures at all:

> *"As I was actually of the same opinion, but couldn't communicate this openly, I had to try to overcome the resistance and implement the measures to some extent. Of course, we made sure that the measures did not achieve the goals. Ultimately, the whole project didn't have the desired effect."*

The manager stated that the management had spent a lot of money on the consultancy, but the bottom line was that the margin situation had not improved. The project also frustrated the employees.

> *"If the management had formed a core team with its own employees, with a well-founded mandate to look for new sources of margin, there would never have been any resistance, and the employees would have been motivated to get involved."*

Top management fails due to resistance. The union of top management and consultants does not prevail against its opponents from within its own ranks. They assumed that their own people would not have the willingness and perhaps also the competence to cooperate. Their own people therefore felt that their knowledge, their commitment to the company, and their skills were not recognized and not taken seriously.

## Resistance to Preserve One's Freedom

People can react very differently when others try to control, dominate, or govern them. One specific concept that can be directly associated with one-sided, unequally distributed, and dominant power relationships is the concept of reactance (Brehm 1966; Brehm and Brehm 1981). It describes a defensive reaction against a perceived restriction or limitation of personal freedom of choice. Reactance is usually triggered by psychological pressure (e.g. coercion, threats, emotionally charged arguments) or the restriction of freedoms (e.g. bans, new restrictive rules, censorship) and results in an unpleasant state that triggers the impulse to restore these freedoms (Raab et al. 2010, p. 65 et seq.). The person likes the forbidden fruit even more and looks for ways to act out the forbidden behavior anyway. However, the intensity of the reaction varies: the more numerous and important the freedoms are, the more pronounced the reactance not to lose them. Arbitrary, blatant, and direct requests also provoke more reactance than well-founded and sensitively presented requests (Knowles and Linn 2004a, p. 6). The affected person's defensive reaction can manifest itself in open aggression, tactics, a change in attitude, or physiological reactions (Raab et al. 2010, p. 65 et seq.). For example, the person may protest openly or, as in the following example, look for hidden ways to regain lost freedom. The head of the research department of a printing company describes such behavior by an employee and himself with great sympathy:

*"A new fabric was to be printed using a special process. One of my employees was the project manager responsible at the time. The CEO felt that the development progress was insufficient and so he declared the project management to be a matter for the boss and took it upon himself. Depending on progress, he arranged a short review meeting one to three times a week, in which he, the project manager, another employee, and I took part. In an endless, stubborn, and systematic series of tests, over 600 different variations of the print were produced and then jointly assessed. The problem was too complex for a single person to quickly achieve success, whether through diligence or luck. The CEO experimented himself in his spare time. He made the results available to the project manager for testing purposes but refused to give him any information about the composition. He regularly bypassed me, approached my employee directly and withheld information from me too. The whole thing looked very much like command and obedience. As a trained specialist, he also had a permanent problem with academics, which was probably the real driving force behind his incredible dedication. He always tried to control everything and have a say in everything. The employees were inferior and not worthy of being included. Of course, this also applied to me, as I rarely followed his 'orders.' One day, printed samples were once again evaluated at the review meeting. The CEO asked for another, as yet unprinted copy of a particular sample for further printing trials. The project manager replied that unfortunately he did not have any more samples. The CEO couldn't believe his ears, lost his temper, shouted across the room, and left the building, completely irritated by such 'stupidity.' For a moment, there was a distinct silence amongst those remaining, combined with a certain satisfaction. Then the project manager opened a cupboard containing stacks of fresh, unprinted samples of all previous attempts. He looked at me and said: 'Of course I still have unprinted samples from this trial. But I'm not going to give them to the old man.'"*

The employee refuses the supervisor access to further materials for the test series due to his knowledge advantage.

In doing so, he does not comply with the supervisor's request, even though he knows full well that he could. However, the employee is not simply acting out of base motives according to the favorable assessment of his superior. His behavior is a reaction to a hierarchical, non-transparent and derogatory management or leadership relationship. The employee pays back the superior one-to-one: opaqueness is answered with opaqueness. The boss who devalues is devalued, albeit not directly, as an outmoded idiot. The hierarchical intervention and the associated loss of autonomy as well as the presumed offense on the part of the employee are punished with sabotage. The employee thus has many "good reasons" to let the boss run riot and even receives appreciative approval from his direct superior, the narrator. The employee is obviously disrupting work processes, but is that not understandable? At the end of the narrative, the manager has a reasoned argument:

> *"This situation has made it clear to me that absolute control is neither possible nor sensible. In such a constellation, every employee will look for ways to take back the freedom to which they are entitled."*

A good example of reactance.

## Resistance as an Emotional Event

In the context of work, we are used to evoking certain emotions, whether we feel that way or not. A waiter is expected to be friendly and smile, a project manager is expected to be enthusiastic about a new project. If people do not feel these emotions, suppress true feelings, and display false emotions this can be described as superficial behavior. We observed this, for example, in employees who applauded management on the surface but then strongly opposed management in an informal setting (see section 3.2). However, depending on the job, not expressing one's own emotions directly is not only very helpful, but also a necessary skill for performance. This emotional work can be illustrated by an incident described by a telephone operator at a US emergency call center (Shuler and Sypher 2000, p. 76): a female student called in a panic because she found herself, all alone, confronted by a spider. Instead of scolding her for using the emergency number inappropriately, he answered her calmly:

> *"I said, 'Do you have a textbook, since you're a student?' 'Well, yeah, I do.' 'So, okay, hold the textbook in the corner above where the spider is and drop it and that will kill the spider.' 'Oh, thank you.' She called me back later and said, 'Thanks, thanks. You know it worked; I killed the spider.' She was saying, 'I feel so dumb because I called 911 for that, but I was terrified and didn't know what to do.'"*

But of course, we do not always pretend to be authentic in management situations, where this is highly appreciated. In situations of resistance, however, the rules of the game change, as good or learned intentions do not always work in situations that are perceived as unusual. The people involved are usually emotionally agitated, even if you cannot see it in the person's face. Alternatively, emotions are brought to the surface, are visible, and the other person is surprised by them. In resistance situations, the strong feelings relate to decisions, behavior, specific events, communicated beliefs, or specifically against people: anger, contempt, enthusiasm, envy, fear, frustration, disappointment, embarrassment, indignation, happiness, hatred, envy, joy, love, pride, surprise, and sadness (Robins and Judge 2013, p. 100).

The intensity of emotions varies depending on the situation and is visible or accessible. Nevertheless, a fundamental area of tension arises. This is because management is traditionally equated with rationality. It is expected not to be guided or carried away by emotions. In some of the cases of resistance described in this book, strong emotions, which tend to be negative, are not immediately devalued, but understood as a vehement and justified articulation of concrete concerns. In many cases, however, as we have seen, negative emotions are attributed to the resisters or negative emotions are attached to their behavior and thus devalued. The expectation is placed on the management, which is then confronted with resistance, not to react emotionally (as well). However, if the management does not react emotionally, but rather in a cool and distanced manner, to emotional impulses in the organization and imposes its ideas on the organization or individual members, this is likely to be perceived as threatening by the members of the organization. This is because it becomes clear that the management is perceived as inaccessible for the feelings, concerns, or interests of those who are exposed to the changes (Fiol and O'Conner 2002).

This is precisely what can radicalize resistance or contribute to a negative, unproductive resistance dynamic. Fear, anger, or mistrust can then no longer be dismissed as natural reactions to all changes. Rather, it becomes clear that these are very specific responses or reactions to management behavior. And these reactions can mobilize strong collective forces for resistance, especially when the moral consequences of the changes or decisions are challenged. Resistance becomes a tense activity that is passionate and driven by emotion: resistors may appear aggressive, disobey rules, pick fights, attempt to undermine authority, ignore new impositions, or begin to sabotage (LaNuez and Jermier 1994; Sturdy and Fineman 2001). However, this is not to deny legitimacy to the demands, concerns, or complaints that lie behind the strong and usually negatively perceived feelings of managers. It should simply be recognized that strong and negative emotions are often displayed in situations of resistance. Dealing with this productively means understanding the anger, rage, or disappointment shown as a form of expression of commitment to a cause and to the organization and not as a means of pressure or power against the management.

It has long been known in research that emotions are crucial for rational, reason-oriented thinking. Consider the case of Phineas Gage, a railroad worker from Vermont. He is considered one of the most famous patients in the history of neuroscience. On a September day in 1848, Gage was supposed to drill holes in rocks, fill them with gunpowder, and then plug them with sand. When he rammed the tamping iron into a borehole, a spark caused the powder to explode. The tamping iron entered his head below the left eye, passed through the left frontal lobe of his brain, exited the skull just next to the vertex line, and flew about 20 meters farther. However, Gage remained conscious. A doctor later determined that brain matter with the volume of "a half-filled teacup" had been lost. Phineas Gage survived, but the terrible accident led to noticeable personality changes. The previously friendly and even tempered Gage became an impulsive and unreliable person. He began to make irrational decisions, behaving erratically and acting against his own interests. This example illustrates that the ability to make rational decisions is linked to emotional abilities. Emotions make organizations come alive (Fineman 2006, p. 675), they flow into everyday life and shape it. Perceptions, decisions, statements, and reactions are always influenced by emotions. Reason requires emotions, in contrast to the common belief that emotions stand in the way of rationality. This is because emotions provide us with information about how to understand the world around us (Robins and Judge 2013, p. 102 et seq.). Accordingly, emotional reactions, regardless of whether they are perceived as positive or negative, convey new information about management relationships, past interactions, misunderstandings, failures, or even mistakes. Recognizing emotions as a means of expression and not suppressing them indicates that we should engage with the other person even better and more authentically.

## 6.3 Resistance to Control and Appropriation by the Organization

In section 6.1 we looked at explanatory models at the level of the individual and in section 6.2 at those that relate to relationships between people. In this section 6.3 and the following section 6.4, we will move to the organizational level and look at tendencies and dynamics in organizations that also explain how resistance can be justified. In this section, I will look at how organizations exert undue influence on the people working for them, thus triggering resistance. On the one hand, this influence is exerted in a bureaucratic, technical way, but also through the norms that apply in the organization.

### Resistance to Bureaucratic and Technical Control

Control in organizations serves either to verify the desired goals and thus the correctness of the strategy ("doing the right things") or – at the operational level – the achievement of goals ("doing things right"). Control is an organized function. Even with self-organization and self-control procedures, there are usually forms of external control, which is bureaucratic and carried out, for example, with the help of guidelines, defined procedures, job and activity descriptions, and regulated documentation. People, their development, activities, and work results are thus subjected to scrutiny. Bureaucratic control is supported and supplemented by technical control (i.e. by standardized, usually IT-supported instruments and procedures) (Ashforth and Mael 1998, p. 92). The control between the manager and the employees brings the bureaucratic and technical control to life, but may also weaken it, relativize it ("We handle it differently here"), or reinforce it through further behavior ("I want you to inform me about every further step"). Nevertheless, employees are not necessarily expected to really believe in what they are doing. They have to follow the rules and do the work, and this is checked with the help of external control.

Organizations tend to introduce formal rules to ensure a competent, reliable process or to avoid errors. However, they also use increasingly sophisticated IT and data processing programs to improve control. Wherever possible, performance can be recorded, discussed, and problematized on an ongoing basis, including individually.

The 2011 documentary *Work Hard Play Hard* by director Carmen Losmann deals with new forms of work organization and methods of personnel management. In a "lean" project at the logistics company DHL, processes are to be made more efficient. An incident is documented in which the supervisor enters an open-plan office and calls the employees together. Every day, key figures are recorded on a performance board and shown to the employees. At the end of the meeting, the manager comments on the key figures as follows:

> *"We had a total of 1,228 contacts yesterday. That's good. We created a total of 1,012 cases on FP6 in SAP, 377 closed, making 37.25 percent first level. Still at a high level. Any comments, notes, or questions about yesterday's figures? Thank you, happy working."*

At the beginning of the conversation with the employees, the line manager asks how things are going. "Good" is the first shy answer. When asked how it went yesterday, the following dialog takes place:

> *Employee with a mischievous smile: "I feel better." "Why?" The employee laughs and then says bluntly: "Because I wasn't here." The line manager comments dryly: "Good for you, bad for us."*

The humorous, slightly cynical statements reveal the subtle resistance of employees to the system, which is geared toward tight control. No loud rebellion against the control system can be detected, as this form of control cannot be traced back directly to individuals but is simply an expression of progressive rationalization in the world of work, in this case specifically in the service sector. It is technically possible and that is why the company makes full use of the technical possibilities. The individual distances himself from what is happening with humor or cynicism, otherwise resigning himself to his fate for lack of alternatives.

However, this process of progressive control can lead to open resistance if an initiator for the increasingly sophisticated IT-supported management techniques is recognizable. A manager from the administration department of a hospital reported that employees in the outpatient billing department were increasingly complaining that there was little feedback from their direct supervisor on suggestions for improvement and change and that these were "fizzling out." At this point, the manager intended to introduce new, weekly key figures that would provide information about the performance of the department as well as that of each individual employee. Her intention was:

> *"From my point of view, the non-anonymized key figures should also encourage discussions within the team (including with superiors) and, of course, improve performance."*

In particular, the fact that the key figures were not anonymized met with great resistance:

> *"On the one hand, I could (partly) understand the employees' arguments (such as bad for team spirit etc.). However, I was of the opinion that it was precisely these key figures that offered the platform to take a (more) detailed look at the workflows and processes of the operational business. In addition, they also provided clear arguments as*

*to why someone was able to achieve more in a certain period than someone else in the team ..."*

In the end, the manager realizes that she had to do much more convincing to persuade the employees of the benefits of the key figures than she had originally imagined.

The manager's report describes a stage on the way to progressive rationalization of the organization. Managerial control is to be expanded. From the point of view of the narrator, it is an instrument for increasing productivity, which was not possible with the previous communicative procedures. It also allows transparency and justifiability in the event of unequal performance. From the other perspective, the focus is now on the performance of the individual and not that of the collective. The measurement logic is based on the idea that collective performance is the sum of individual performance. Employees fear that the new measurement method will motivate individuals to improve their performance at the expense of the collective to avoid the risk of sanctions. However, it is also conceivable that employees will resist the fact that the organization is now able to control them directly and immediately. They may gain the impression that they are now permanently available to the organization without any fluctuations in performance and that they must constantly justify their (slightly) fluctuating performance.

At the end, the manager sums up:

*"In the meantime, the whole thing has proven itself and is no longer questioned."*

What happened to the resistance? Has the resistance been overcome or broken or has the superior been convinced? We can only make assumptions here: it is conceivable that the resistance died down or was no longer audible or visible to the manager, but this does not suggest that the individuals have seen the superior's argument, but that they have simply given up their open resistance to the advancing rationality of the organization. It is also possible that the instrument was not used at all and therefore had no effect on day-to-day management.

## Resistance to Normative Control

For less-privileged activities, the work simply has to be done: the metal sheet must be punched correctly, the apartment must be neatly cleaned, and the hamburger must be finished in the allotted time. Knowledge workers, on the other hand, should also enjoy their work and see it as a fun experience. In today's organizations, organizational control goes one step further. Not only are correct behaviors expected, but also the right attitudes, mindsets, motivations, or emotions. Bureaucratic and technical control are supplemented by normative control and all three forms of control can occur simultaneously (Schutz 2004, p. 15 et seq.). The employee must be wholeheartedly committed to the company. Swiss Post, for example, focuses on "emotionalization" in its top management training. The aim is to enable managers to better navigate the area of tension between political and entrepreneurial demands by strengthening their personal impact in this dual role with passion, inspiration, and agility. With positive and empowering emotions, managers should be able to move the organization forward by taking responsibility and "effectively creating a sense of something new" amongst employees. These new action-guiding emotions are themselves conveyed in an emotionalized manner to generate attention (Athanassov 2014, p. 6). Very specific emotions are to be awakened, taught, and conveyed within the company, with the idea that managers will adopt these emotions and act accordingly. New and empowering emotions should be built into the manager, so to speak.

In the documentary mentioned above, a Unilever company slogan is quoted: "We are Unilever. Go for it." At Unilever, the individual is not just a worker who delivers his or her performance. You have to commit to the company as a whole person, with your experiences, thoughts, and feelings, and become part of an enthusiastic and inspiring community. The documentary gives further examples that illustrate this. Unilever was planning a new building for Unilever DACH (Germany, Austria, Switzerland) in Hamburg. As part of the construction project, the company sent architectural firms tender documents from which an architect read out the objectives for the building:

> *"The choice to construct a new building in HafenCity, the one place in Hamburg that stands for modernity and dynamism, fits in perfectly with Unilever's objectives. Because these attributes, modern and dynamic, are to be consistently continued in the new building to be erected with the means of architectural and interior design – as a sign of the departure into a modern and dynamic future. The building is to be an architectural highlight for the Unilever brand and, as an innovative building, embody the new spirit of the vital company and the team concept of 'One Unilever.' Well-lit and transparent offices are not intended to convey fun at work through luxury, but through a vitalizing and functional appearance, color, materials, nature, and worlds of experience."*

The architect is very pleased that the company describes a "working atmosphere," an "emotional world" that it "wants to see generated" in the building. Another architect reflects:

> *"With the reprogramming, with a new building, you have synergy effects. This means that the operating structures suddenly change with a new building. Everything is put to the test. And the fact that you have everything in one building and everything is highly communicative and flexible changes the entire corporate culture. In other words, the new culture and the new building are mutually dependent."*

The architects further reflect that the building should convey that:

*"work doesn't have to be a constraint. It should never be a place where I am reminded to work."*

Work must be fun and fulfilling, and employees are offered an infrastructure that aims to give people precisely this feeling. Inside the imposing new Unilever building, Harry Brouwer, the Dutch executive vice president of Unilever DACH from 2009 to 2014, gave a speech that included the following words:

*"We know what we want to achieve this year. But we also know how we want to achieve it: with a culture, a spirit, and a mega-growth mentality. We want to win in the market, which means doubling our business on a global level. So – very ambitious overall. Basically, we know what we want to achieve, together, each of us in our work plan, each of us in our team. And together, we are Unilever. Go for it."*

Every Wednesday evening at 6 p.m., the Unilever management team meets to go spinning together in the company's fitness center. The management came up with this idea together – after all, they all need to be fit. Of course, they also talk about work, but the training is primarily about having fun (Heintze 2010). However, there are also other unconventional methods shown in the documentary to get employees to put their heart and soul into the organization and the team. A group completes management and team training in the climbing park. Shortly before jumping off a platform in the climbing park, each participant commits to a personal mission statement, such as the following:

*"I will soon be working even harder and learning a lot in a short space of time so that I can support my team even better."*

A line manager commits himself to making his employees even more committed:

*"In the near future, I will demand more of the whole group, to enable concentrated work. Sometimes it's easy for everyone to work on their own. It really is better, as we learned today, to tackle things together, even if it can be exhausting."*

Finally, the participants stand on a platform from which they are attached to a winch and jump a few meters into the depths. One participant admits weaknesses and commits to improving:

*"I will listen more to my colleagues' problems in the future because I know that if I deal with my colleagues' problems, I can get them involved. Because I can respond to them."*

Once at the bottom, he reports:

*"It's an incredible feeling to put yourself in the arms of your colleagues, so to speak, to let yourself go. It's a very, very nice feeling and I'm happy to be able to spend all my time working with you … doing this every day."*

What happens here? The employee must show his or her personal weaknesses or weaknesses identified as such by superiors or colleagues, humbly admit them, and then exchange them for new characteristics that are more functional from the company's point of view. The example of Unilever shows that the organization expects individuals to adapt their self-image and identity to that of the company and to be emotionally closely connected to the company. This normative control is no longer an external control, but an internal control which, and this is the perfidious thing about it, makes it appear to be freely chosen (Ashforth and Mael 1998, p. 93). The individual merges with the organization.

In Chapter 4, we learned about the example of the management consultancy Magnum, whose standards were so strongly internalized by the employees that any attempts at resistance could not even be detected or were immediately neutralized. This was not ensured by a higher authority, but by the fact that the norms developed their effectiveness within the individual.

However, we have also seen many examples of organizational members resisting this normative colonization, for example through humor or cynicism (section 3.1 and section 3.2). These forms of resistance subtly bring inadequacies, inappropriateness, or problems to the surface and can thus thwart or kibosh the intentions of management (Westwood 2004), and the resisters retain the feeling of remaining free and themselves. Resistance is thus directed against the progressive expansion of management and control attempts (Cunha et al. 2013, p. 468).

Under the smooth surface of the organizational fun society, however, questionable behavior can also creep in, which management would never formally stand by, but informally condones. Management tolerates it or makes it taboo in a calculating way. And some members of the organization can then oppose this questionable behavior. One example is the Australian call center Sunray (Fleming 2007). Since the activities at a call center tend to be simple and monotonous, management decided to make Sunray a fun, joyful, fulfilling place to work. The boundaries between work and leisure blurred as there was no formal dress code and employees came to work in their leisure clothes, just as they went out in the evening after work. The company's management tacitly approved of its members living out their sexuality more or less openly. Sunray was considered a sexually charged place, a stimulating environment in which to meet other women and men, flirt, or even have an affair. There were heterosexuals working at Sunray, but just as many homosexuals. One team leader summed up the culture at Sunray as follows:

*"We like to think of ourselves as fun, sexy, and dedicated."*

Many heterosexual men appreciated this sexually charged atmosphere, whereas some women felt uncomfortable and harassed and derogatorily used the term "meat market." Men who distanced themselves from it referred to those women who got involved as "sluts" and men as "sleazy, disgusting types." Particularly obscene terms were used for gay men. Sunray's critical employees were convinced that the company wanted employees to adopt a false, superficial, or simple-minded personality to maintain the fun culture and thus productivity.

The case reveals that a sexually charged, masculine culture was established under the surface of the "fun organization," which was condoned and tolerated by management because it served the purpose of maintaining or increasing productivity. One group of employees felt liberated and could live out their needs. Another group, on the other hand, perceived this "freedom" as a nuisance. The resistance was not fundamentally directed against the fun organization, but against varied interpretation of fun. Employees resisted the underground phenomenon of sexualization because they felt harassed and controlled by an intrusive, monopolizing organization. The resistance was expressed in understandable rejection of the harassment, but also in extremely derogatory, sometimes homophobic condemnations.

## 6.4 Resistance Due to Cultural Routines Within the Organization

Whilst in section 6.1 we dealt with the individual and in section 6.2 with the relationships between people, both the previous and this section deal with the level of the organization. Whilst section 6.3 dealt with both bureaucratic and normative control as a cause of resistance, we now look at the culture of the organization as a cause of resistance in organizations.

The norms, which we looked at in more detail in the previous section, influence the members in such a way that they behave in a way that makes resistance unlikely. The normative control of the organization thus increasingly neutralizes resistance. By contrast, this section deals with very specific cultural characteristics of organizations that provoke resistance. To this end, I would first like to clarify the understanding of organizations as cultural entities on which this section is based.

Organizations are micro societies in which people perform their tasks in defined roles to achieve the organization's collective goals. As in society, formal and informal rules exist in the organization. For example, the organization has management manuals, working time regulations, and financial guidelines. They are observed or disregarded, interpreted differently, forgotten, or circumvented – sometimes more and sometimes less consciously. There are also informal rules, values, and standards that shape the way we live together to a considerable extent. And it is precisely in this informal dimension of the organization, as I will show below, that the causes of resistance lie.

It is a somewhat peculiar idea that common, collective patterns in organizations shape the actions of individuals (i.e. that these are not completely self-determined). The cultural view of organizations assumes that organizations define certain courses of action in their culture, which the members then follow. In a study conducted at the University of Zurich, the professional category of "banker" was examined more closely. This is against the backdrop of the fact that there have been repeated cases of fraud in recent years, some of them on a massive scale, which has severely damaged the image of the entire banking sector and thus also that of bank employees. The question now was whether "bank employees are less honest people by nature." The study showed that bank employees are no more dishonest in their free time than employees in other professions. But as soon as they take on their professional role, they behave more dishonestly than employees in other professions. In the banking sector, there are obviously very specific norms that lead to dishonest behavior being tolerated (Cohn et al. 2014). In this respect, it is crucial to understand the specific organizational cultures more precisely to be able to see behind the concrete and observable behaviors and thus also behind the resistance behavior in order to draw appropriate conclusions.

However, one should be careful not to prematurely qualify or devalue the culture of an organization as inherently resistant or stolid, for example. Organizational culture can paralyze or promote developments; it can lead to resistance having destructive, but also equally invigorating and constructive effects. Organizational culture is not an object that can be modeled, manipulated, or reconfigured by managers independently of themselves. It is created and shaped by all system members in their day-to-day management and work. "They follow a script, so to speak, which they continuously create together without explicitly writing it down. The script is not immediately apparent to observers, whether external or internal" (Baitsch and Nagel 2014, p. 272). But that's not all: modesty and, ideally, a certain serenity are appropriate regarding the possibilities of shaping the culture of an organization. This is because culture cannot be precisely controlled by management (or by other members of the organization). Instead, it is better to speak of a shared and reciprocal shaping or development of culture. This may sound somewhat abstract at first glance, so here is a brief example: trust is not simply created through (supposed or intended) trusting gestures by a manager or an employee. Trust is created or lost – like all cultural characteristics of an organization – in interrelated behavior. Trust cannot be brought about unilaterally, but only arises when the actors perceive each other's actions as trusting and trustworthy. It is usually not clear exactly how the trust came about, but it is also irrelevant (Baitsch and Nagel 2014, p. 272).

Organizational culture offers "aids to perception and interpretation, i.e. it spans a horizon of meaning for the actors that gives them reliable information about what is relevant in the organization and what can be neglected, what is considered the right and wrong view, what may be done and what should be avoided if possible" (Baitsch 1993). It allows me to find my way in everyday working life, gives me security and a reliable orientation as to how I have to deal with new information or whether the organization is interested in it at all. The culture thus defines "valid, largely implicit paths of action" (Baitsch 1998), as was observed, for example, at the Sunray call center (see section 6.3) or the Magnum management consultancy (see Chapter 4).

A well-known phenomenon in organizations is that different departmental logics, such as those of marketing, controlling, or human resources, or those of staff and operational units, seem to clash irreconcilably. The cultural characteristic of the entire organization is then not the unifying factor. Instead, a look at the culture reveals that the members are working against each other and why. People talk past each other, see the problem in a different place or not at all, or disagree about the usefulness of the proposed measures. These are not simply factual differences, but rather fundamental professional understandings and assumptions about how events in and around the organization should be viewed and shaped. I would like to point this out in advance: these different points of view are of crucial importance for the performance of the organization, but they can also completely block up the organization, with some putting up massive resistance to others. Let us take an example from a hospital where the hospital director thinks about the relationship with doctors and a chief physician thinks about hospital directors (Endrissat et al. 2007):

> *One hospital director reports: "But of course it is a permanent – I say permanent – struggle. Because for them [the chief physicians], the increased integration [of tasks and processes] that I initiated has led to a loss of autonomy in some cases, and [autonomy] naturally goes hand in hand with prestige."*
>
> *A chief physician reports: "If you put a CEO in front of me, I'll turn into the most horrible troublemaker you can imagine. I can guarantee that. Because I can't accept someone who doesn't understand the subject matter simply leading in a dictatorial manner ... I accept people who understand their subject matter; who rationally say: 'So yes, so no.' But people who give me the feeling that they have no idea what they're talking about – I don't accept that."*

CEO management structures have been introduced in many Swiss hospitals. The hospital manager alone bears overall responsibility for the hospital and no longer shares this with a medical director. Things become difficult when hospital managers want to assert their claim to lead the chief physicians. This is clearly a clash between two professional groups with very different understandings of management. Hospital managers see themselves as responsible for the whole and have to simplify and integrate the complex professional organization, which is strongly focused on operative cases. To achieve this, they have to give their concerns weight and acceptance and also stand up for the overarching interests of the hospital.

Chief physicians, on the other hand, represent the actual core business of the hospital: they save lives and restore people to health. They focus on their discipline and the specific surgical case and not on the institution. Accordingly, management means something different. According to the doctors' understanding of management, they have to deploy and educate their staff. Medical managers see it as their task to further develop the professionalism of the doctors assigned to them by imparting knowledge, skills, attitudes, and values to them in practice or by providing the framework for them to acquire these. They are entitled to do this because they have acquired superior qualifications and hold the corresponding position. And it is precisely from this that the claim to autonomy is derived, which they see as being jeopardized by structural and economic developments. To a certain extent, the CEO is the symbolic and addressable representative of this development (Endrissat and Müller 2007). Against this background, it should come as no surprise that a CEO accuses the chief physicians of resistance and, conversely, the chief physicians accuse the CEO of the same resistance.

However, resistance results not only from the different norms or professional understandings within an organization, but also from the existing cultural and shared characteristics of the organization. We consider this in the case of the introduction of private sector management methods (new public management) in public administration. In a cantonal administration in Switzerland, pilot offices were selected for each department (ministry). The start was euphoric and those involved had high hopes for what was to come. A project organization was set up so that the pilot offices could now effectively break new ground. The view prevailed that the heads of the pilot offices were independent entrepreneurs and should therefore know how to implement "new public management." The heads of the pilot offices soon made it clear that they would like to commission an external consultant to tell them "which rolls we have to bake." However, the management team did not respond.

During the long initial phase, it was not possible to agree on a reform program or joint steps. Lethargy set in. Finally, the management team agreed that the heads of the pilot offices should present their results. The results proved to be completely heterogeneous. Everything seemed to be drifting apart. The reform project threatened to be a failure. The hierarchy was quickly reactivated, assignments distributed, and control groups introduced. The management consultant who was then brought in was welcomed as the savior, as he now set out the program in three easy-to-understand steps. At first, the heads of the pilot offices were delighted because something was finally happening. But time was now running out. Individual orders could not be fulfilled, and reminders were issued to complete them, as the milestones had to be met at all costs. Individual pilot offices became extremely stressed. Finally, there was an open protest in which the head of a pilot office vented his anger as follows:

> *"We are responsible for that ourselves. We're not going to allow ourselves to be talked into it and simply bombarded with deadlines. The employees are already at the limit anyway. (...) Besides, new public management is not our hobby, and we still have to do our daily work."*

How can this episode and the resulting resistance be understood from a cultural perspective? Typically, it is not the task of public administration to develop new rules itself. We expect the public administration to implement the rules that have come about democratically. But in this very project, it would have been necessary to define new rules (of new public management) themselves. However, this contradicted the prevailing cultural norm of rule orientation and rule enforcement. The room for maneuver was reinterpreted as a vacuum of rules, which makes it easier to understand the described lethargy that initially set in. The logic of rule enforcement also implies a logic of error avoidance. Against this background, the heterogeneity of the results was not interpreted as a source of learning, but as an error, and thus the bureaucratic logic trap of error-free rule implementation snapped shut. The mistakes or supposed failures could have been attributed to the project team, so they tried to deflect responsibility away from themselves by reorganizing. Right from the start, but also with the appearance of the consultant, others defined the rules and not those who could have designed the new rules. The originally empowered pilot office managers thus relinquished all creative options. The implementation of the program was ensured through hierarchical control. The irony of fate: those who had demanded the rules and their implementation were the ones who fought against these rules and their implementation. The cat chased its own tail. This example shows how resistance is rooted in the traditional cultural norms of the organization.

However, resistance can also be seen as a potentially productive element of the organizational culture. In such a culture, resistance can mean that members have the courage to defend themselves against unreasonable demands or what they see as wrong decisions by management, as we saw in the bank case study (see section 2.1). But this requires a relationship of trust in management relationships, as all those involved recognize that they can sometimes be wrong. In such learning-oriented cultures (Müller and Hurter 1999), differing assessments, values, or the specific concerns of others are recognized and accepted and the search for a good solution begins.

The culture of an organization develops and consolidates over time. Knowing this and tracking down the cultural patterns and dynamics is fruitful: the cultural perspective offers a deeper understanding of why organizational members or entire organizations act, behave, perform, and (do not) develop in this way and not differently. It is therefore a matter of assigning meaning to everyday management situations or to routines that are constantly repeated. And this can lead to very different conclusions:

- **Mutual Recognition:** resistance arises due to very fundamental and seemingly irreconcilable and conflicting views
and values. In the mode of either-or, one's own point of view
tends to be seen as superior and that of others as inferior.
The task of management is to initiate a process with the aim
of mutual recognition and appreciation of perspectives and
the exploration of a common understanding of management
and organization.

- **Mode Compatibility:** resistance brings to light cultural
patterns that prove to be dysfunctional when implementing
the reform program. This does not mean that the focus on
rules and the avoidance of errors should generally be called
into question. Rather, this organization should be aware that
a new logic of learning is needed in addition to the bureaucratic logic and that it must be continuously clarified which
mode is functional in the respective situation or how both
modes can be compatible with each other.

From a cultural perspective, it is clear that resistance arises
from familiar, self-evident and, above all, jointly established
routines which can become permanently entrenched. Here too,
indignation about the backwardness or inertia of an organizational culture is tantamount to a blanket devaluation. It must be
acknowledged that organizations have built up these routines
over the years and that the members stick to them because the
routines are the way they are. They are the reality of the organization and individuals cannot simply opt out. Power games, a
lack of customer proximity, an orientation toward rules rather
than freedom, a lack of self-confidence in being able to assert
oneself in the market, or over-optimism on the part of managers (Lovallo and Kahneman 2003) – all of these are essentially
ingrained cultural characteristics of the organization that are

no longer questioned. All these collective characteristics of the organization cannot be remedied by the individual employee simply seeing the world differently or being a little more courageous. Rather, it is important to simply acknowledge them and better understand the reasons for these collective patterns instead of blaming and even devaluing a certain group of people in the organization. After all, the entire organization has contributed to these patterns, which also means that all members of the organization must contribute to changing or developing the patterns.

## Summary

- There are various approaches that seek to explain the forms of expression, origins, and courses of resistance situations and processes, and contribute to a better understanding of resistance.

- Resistance in organizations cannot be explained by certain characteristics or behaviors of individuals, but rather by the relationship dynamics between people and the norms and culture of the organization.

- At an individual level, it becomes clear that resistance is not a consistent attitude. Members of organizations are not simply against something. Their attitudes toward change or decisions are often complex, contradictory, or ambivalent. Moreover, these attitudes can change over time.

- If we look at resistance as an interpersonal phenomenon, it becomes clear that it arises from a mostly unproductive relationship dynamic between the people involved and is an expression of a damaged relationship, however that may be.

- Both bureaucratic and normative control can cause resistance, whereas normative control specifically can also lead to the organization immunizing itself against resistance, as explained in Chapter 4.

- A cultural view of an organization also helps elucidate why resistance arises, why it can become entrenched in a destructive way, or how it can be dealt with in a constructive manner.

CHAPTER

# 7

# Leadership: The Art of Dealing Productively with Resistance

The senses do not deceive because they do not judge at all.
—Immanuel Kant

If we now focus on leadership, we must first define it. Leadership is not a characteristic, not a behavior, but a form of shaping relationships that are generally hierarchical. All those involved have an influence on the leadership process and the leadership relationship (Müller and Widmer 1989). Dealing with resistance is therefore not simply a matter for the manager; rather, all those involved contribute to a greater or lesser extent to constructive or destructive resistance dynamics. However, if we then assume that one of the tasks of management is to cultivate a constructive

191

work and management culture, then it has a special responsibility in shaping resistance situations.

Having dealt with the manifestations of resistance and the mostly unquestioned assumptions and dynamics, and having established time and again that dealing with resistance rarely takes a productive course, in this final chapter we will explore the question of what a constructive or productive approach to resistance means and how this can be achieved. However, we must refrain from the idea that we can now analyze all situations involving resistance in a razor-sharp and conclusive manner and thus get a better grip on them.

There are two main reasons for this: firstly, resistance situations are inherently complex and therefore challenging to understand, and they often remain at least somewhat enigmatic. Secondly, everyday organizational and management life happens quickly before our eyes, and individuals cannot simply remove themselves from this stream of events to reflect on the situation for an hour with a coach but are required to behave in one way or another. It's like catching trout with your bare hands: the moment we think we've caught the fish, it slips out of our hands. But even if this is the case, we can approach resistance in other ways. That is what this chapter is about. As paradoxical as it may sound, the increase in our ability to act comes from the fact that we realize that we cannot recognize and understand everything. This uncertainty must be acknowledged and if this insight is present, it is also easier to live with it.

When dealing with resistance, we must not fall into the trap of assuming that it is always good and justified: "To put it crudely, not all resistance is good" (Fleming 2007, p. 252). Neither a one-sided partisanship for the resisters or insurgents nor a clear position for the managers helps. Just as the manager is not always right and behaves correctly, the content of resistance is not always justified, and its form is not always appropriate. The crux of the matter is that this cannot be judged a priori or hastily but requires a conscientious (self-)examination.

Before we look more specifically at the question of how to deal constructively with resistance, I think it is imperative that I clarify my own position by outlining the basic working assumptions. I believe that it helps to have an orienting idea of how to handle organization and relationships in organizations. In section 7.1, I develop four interlocking leadership principles (commitment, dignity, right to dissent, and learning) that are particularly important in situations of resistance. I then illustrate the relevance of these four principles using what I consider to be a very carefully constructed leadership case in section 7.2. In the last two sections, 7.3 and 7.4, I develop design recommendations for management in dealing with resistance. On the one hand, this is about how managers can deal with resistance when they are confronted with it, but also when they themselves create resistance.

## 7.1 Four Leadership Principles

The discussion of resistance so far in this book can be summarized in four very basic management principles that need to be considered when dealing with resistance:

1. **Commitment:** Managers see themselves as part of what is happening in front of their eyes. They are not simply silent observers but see their part in the situation and try to shape the relationships productively to the best of their knowledge and belief.

2. **Dignity:** In situations of resistance, those involved run the risk of violating or even destroying the dignity of other people. The main task of management is not to turn people in organizations into victims, but to give them the role of doers.

3. **Right to dissent:** An essential and repeatedly observed origin for the emergence of resistance is that dissent is seen as a disruptive factor that disturbs the order and has a destabilizing effect. A new understanding of organizations in general is probably required here if the right to dissent is fundamentally granted to those affected within the organization.

4. **Learning:** The hasty conclusions presented in Chapter 5 may bring more certainty but provide little insight into what happened. Individuals or groups are treated stereotypically and devalued. This perspective is contrasted with a forward-looking and learning-oriented attitude.

In my view, none of these four leadership principles should be put up for discussion or subordinated to another. For example, the development of the organization must not take place at the expense of political requirements. Managers must be committed to relationships so that the right to dissent does not become an empty phrase. In addition, humane treatment within the organization must always be guaranteed. Are these lofty claims? They may be, but why should management not accept this challenge if it proves useful and expedient in situations of resistance?

## Commitment

The forms of resistance presented in linear succession in Chapters 2–4 may obscure the fact that everyday management and organizational life and very specific situations often present themselves as ambiguous. Everyday life is chaotic, as events, changes, and constellations of people constantly overlap. This also means that different forms of resistance exist at any given time and that this resistance can also relate to different things. "Resistance" is not an objective finding, but rather an interpretation, as some attribute resistance to others. Resistance therefore always arises from the relationship, from shared stories between people or groups. It is part of the often complex and stressful relationship dynamics experienced by those involved.

People in organizations navigate this terrain daily, even if they do not encounter resistance every day. It is obviously a challenging task for managers to recognize this resistance in the first place, then to organize it appropriately and to respond to it in a suitable manner. However, we should not be satisfied with the realization: "Look, this is probably resistance." This would reflect a distanced, diagnostic attitude: as if the doctor is observing the patient in expectation and in the knowledge of deficits. As if a spectator were watching the sad spectacle of employees or colleagues on the stage of everyday life. A manager thus remains in the position of an uninvolved observer instead of, as would be more appropriate, acting. And this movement goes in the direction of the person offering resistance. Peter Bieri (2013, p. 99 et seq.) uses the appropriate term "committed encounter." He says "you are not indifferent to what the other person does and experiences. You are not insensible. It doesn't have to be about pleasant, consensual things. There are also committed encounters with anger and hatred." Engagement means recognizing that you are a part of and sharing actively in the situation and taking this role seriously, even if it is unpleasant and comes at an inappropriate time. Beyond acknowledging this, it means that I am actively involved.

As the various cases and experiences of resistance in this book show, the actors have a strong tendency to seek explanations quickly and conclusively for what they find in the situation. This is particularly understandable because the situations are difficult to decipher and emotionally charged. However, the management world is then divided into the diagnostic explainer and those whose behavior is being explained. This can also easily be done with the help of the explanatory models listed in Chapter 6.

They can also be used to grasp the situation hastily and explain it conclusively.

If we start from the concept of *understanding* instead, then this suggests the attitude that you want to grasp the meaning as comprehensively as possible, and this requires that one really takes a close look at the situation beforehand. However, it can also happen that we don't understand everything or only parts of it. When dealing with resistance, a committed encounter is about understanding more precisely what is going on. You begin the journey of exploration, find new clues, surprising or familiar things, reassemble the findings, and remain open to new insights. I see this attitude as the basis for the further considerations that follow.

## Dignity

The cases and findings in this book so far show that excessive restrictions on autonomy and self-determination can lead to resistance in very different forms – be it in the form of resignation, subtle sabotage, or open opposition. The restriction of the individual's self-determination is usually imposed by the hierarchy. It is authorized to persuade subordinates to do something, to order or impose something on them, or to force them to do something. As workers, people become a means or instrument to achieve an end (Bieri 2013, p. 27). A certain degree of subordination, dependence, and independence in working management and leadership relationships is not only functional but is also accepted. Due to this right of control over people, however, the management or the organization also has the duty to ensure that people in organizations remain a "relatively autonomous actor" "instead of becoming simply the means" (Crozier and Friedberg 1993, p. 17). The authority over other people must therefore maintain and respect a certain degree of autonomy or self-determination, because otherwise the person is merely an object or instrument in the hands of others. What happens if management does not strike the right balance and restricts autonomy and independence too much? If people are patronized, incapacitated, paraded, used, abused, humiliated, or feel that way, then their dignity is violated, and they feel robbed of their self-worth.

Resistance situations maneuver everyone involved into a challenging situation that can lead to a violation of dignity. However, preserving dignity is important because it allows the employee to be truly human. People have a right "to be treated in a certain way" (Bieri 2013. p. 11). It is crucial that they are perceived as subjects in the organization and treated as such (Bieri 2013, p. 20 et seq.). They must not, as in some cases described in this book, become exclusively an object or purpose. However, this also means that the individual must perceive themselves as the originator, as the cause of what happens to them and around them. The feeling of causality is not to be equated with claims and fantasies of omnipotence, in which "everything" is attributed to one person. That would bring us back to the hero myths. People must be able to influence events and outcomes together with others (i.e. they must also be granted the right to causality). Otherwise, they become recipients of orders, executors, or subjects, victims of the constraints and decisions of others that affect them. By contrast to this is the role of the "doer," an active person who can help shape things.

The doer influences what concerns him, and now comes the important limitation: as far as this is possible. Because this is not always possible, especially in organizations. If, for example, redundancies have to be announced, managers must become the employees' advocates by first exploring all conceivable options to avert such a decision, and if this is not possible, the people affected must be treated in such a way that their dignity is not lost. They may not have a say in the decision, but the people are not just seen as a means to an end of the organization. Management's credible commitment to them means that they are not just the means. Rather, it is about them as people; they are then seen as an end in themselves. The organization must therefore always be concerned with people, their prospects, hopes, and development during their employment or commitment, even if it has to be terminated. Despite the disappointment of the dismissal, every effort should be made to ensure that the dismissed person can remain a doer (i.e. that they can quickly take control of their future as a person and a worker and does not feel like a victim).

It is precisely in situations of resistance that dignity can come under threat, namely when people feel humiliated by their managers despite knowing better or when the way they are treated seems arbitrary. "Dignity is the right not to be humiliated," writes Peter Bieri (2013, p. 35) aptly. Subjects are independent and think for themselves, which requires that they are not turned into mental followers, but are viewed as responsible beings, which is not the case if decisions are made over their heads and they feel incapacitated and patronized (Bieri 2013, p. 38). If, on the other hand, we assume that people are inert, then we have to patronize them because they do not have the necessary willpower. By contrast, they should be granted an inner independence that allows them to be able to change, to want to change, and not to experience themselves as being chained to the past.

Resistance very often arises when a superior expects and trusts themselves to carry out a thought process, but then no longer trusts the other person affected by the judgment or decision. People then defend themselves against incomprehensible, blind impositions, decisions that cannot be understood or comprehended. Resistance arises when there is no real debate, when there is no serious attempt to put oneself in the other person's shoes (Bieri 2013, p. 98). This gives rise to the demand to grant freedoms: "As long as we have the freedom to make ourselves heard and get involved in the discussion, our dignity is not damaged. That only happens when we are silenced. Only then is paternalism an experience of powerlessness and humiliation" (Bieri 2013, p. 40).

If there is an argument and the other person can make themselves heard, this argument should also be genuine and not just used as social technology. Listening means that what the other person says really sinks in and doesn't just fly past as a babble of words. If the other person wants to make themselves heard, we should also listen properly and put ourselves in the other person's shoes; try to understand and appreciate their arguments, thought processes, and emotional impulses; and then make it clear that we recognize this. This is the only way to create a genuine, authentic, and respectful leadership relationship.

## Right to Dissent

When it comes to the modern image of the organization, new management structures (flat), forms of work (virtual), infrastructures (open-plan office), or cultures (dynamic) are described above all. Perhaps unsurprisingly, the real hot potato is not addressed: the design of power relationships in organizations. There is no question that the organizational principle of hierarchy and vertically distributed responsibilities are functional. However, this also means that the power relationships are often one-sided and any questioning, any criticism becomes a serious threat to order, management, and therefore also to the organization. You can see it that way, but you can also see it quite differently.

I am questioning the one-sided hierarchical model in which "those at the top" always have to know more or know everything better in order to be able to assert themselves in their role. However, it is by no means just the case that management often thinks this way; it is also reflected in the expectation structures of the entire organization. However, this gives rise to the under-standing that management must assert itself, especially when it is met with resistance. Management then becomes unbending, stubborn, and refuses to be swayed from its course. This is how management asserts itself – as a rock in the sea. Some people enjoy this; others experience it as a burden.

Polyarchy, the rule of the many, is known from the disci-pline of politics. If we follow this idea, the political and social structure in the organization and thus the quality of the leader-ship relationship change dramatically. Power relationships are not defined in such a way that it is primarily about having *power over people and resources*, but *power to get things moving*, and not for selfish, defiant reasons. It is not about exercising resistance per se, but about getting things moving – in addition to middle management and top management. The idea of organization is thus moving further and further away from an authoritarian to a democratic regime. What is the value of resistance then? Man-agement processes increasingly resemble dialogs and serious deliberations and consultations. Opposition, objection, counter-opinion, dissent, or challenge – all of these are then part of the official customs in the organization, not because it is about the dispute itself, but because the resisters seriously want to oblige the management to reflect intensively. After all, they are com-petent and have important perspectives, interests, and insights which, in their opinion, are given not enough or no considera-tion and are of great importance for the continued existence and development of the organization. Resistance therefore does not mean influencing the system or the management in such a way that it is weakened or the structural foundations of the organi-zation are damaged. Nor is it about challenging everything and everyone (Courpasson and Clegg 2012).

Instead, a culture of resistance develops in which resistance is permitted and the management and resistors succeed in temporarily suspending the hierarchical power relationship to interact on an equal footing and clarify essential issues. This is not a hot conflict, but rather an open, fair, and mutually respectful exchange of contradictory positions, opinions, and convictions. This does not make the management weak; its strength does not lie in uncompromisingly sticking to its own convictions and decisions, but in listening and leading the communication and interaction processes that then lead to a decision made by the management. Over time, management learns better and better how it can help to avoid some (unnecessarily provoked) resistance. Or to put it another way, management learns better and better how the organization can be intelligently and skillfully involved in decision-making processes without becoming paralyzed.

Resistance in organizations is an organizing concept of management and, as we have seen, usually has negative connotations. Careful handling of the term by management is therefore advisable. The mere statement "you are resisting" or "they are resisting" has consequences. If this "diagnosis" diffuses along winding paths or if management directly confronts those to whom the resistance is attributed, they feel stigmatized, discredited, or even defamed. They then reply indignantly that they are not resisting at all; they just want to be able to speak out because, in their view, management does not have all the relevant information and has made the wrong decision. Or they feel that they are being forced into the role of resistors, which awakens their spirit of resistance; this is when they really put up the barricades. Or they resign themselves, withdraw completely or express their criticism in secret. From this it can be concluded that the term itself should be used with care and that words should be used that describe the observations more precisely: criticism to be taken seriously, differentiated complaint, having the impression that some actions are being made fun of, etc. The type of terms which should be used are those that are not associated with a devaluation of the behavior, but which show that the other person or others have a right to express themselves.

## Learning

Organizations must develop in order to survive. They must identify and develop new markets, develop products and services, and sell them to their customers. This means that the organization must be able to learn and develop. Organizations are confronted with surprises (e.g. a market segment suddenly collapses), experience crises (e.g. sudden appreciation of a currency), or are forced to make interruptions (e.g. violation of environmental protection regulations). However they respond, the best way to face such changes is if (i) the members of the organization feel encouraged to move on and look for new opportunities, provided (ii) they are clear about the direction in which the organization wants to develop. They should also (iii) keep themselves up to date to gain insights into what is happening in the market and in the environment relevant to them. All of this can happen if (iv) management exerts influence to ensure that relationships are respectful and that trusting working relationships can develop (Weick 2000, p. 233).

Dealing with differences and deviations from the norm are particularly important sources of learning. This is the case, for example, when mistakes are made with innovations, when a customer segment sends signals of dissatisfaction, when completely new ideas are introduced into a strategy process or – indeed – when contradictions are voiced. Is this dismissed as irrelevant or interpreted as an unnecessary disruptive signal? Or is it listened to more closely and seriously addressed? We don't want to sing the praises of blue-sky thinkers here, as this role can also become an exhausting process for everyone involved, constantly interrupting the flow of everyday life unnecessarily. Rather, depending on the situation, a constantly rebalanced relationship is required between the continuation of the usual practice and adherence to existing views, between ensuring the necessary stability and the willingness to deviate from it to ensure the necessary flexibility and willingness to adapt. However, it is crucial that the members of the organizations learn to perceive differences in the first place and to address them accordingly. Resistance can arise because organizations find it difficult to allow deviations due to their cultural circumstances, or it can occur when resisters are of the opinion that the organization is not sufficiently responsive.

Accepting that things can turn out differently than you thought is a prerequisite. It means being able to distance yourself from your own opinions, views, and convictions and to acknowledge the existence of something different: How do I see it? How does the other person see it? What assessments do I and the other person make? What is the relationship between the opinions? This makes it possible to gain a new overview of things and to examine alternatives. This does not make me weak, but demonstrates independence in the thought process. Bieri (2013, p. 77) describes this as an "educational process: we learn that there are other standards elsewhere in the world, in other cultures, and we can ask ourselves what we think about them." This means that "our authority is no longer a blind authority," but an authority that is constantly reconstituting itself.

## 7.2 The Four Leadership Principles Illustrated by a Specific Case

What do these four principles mean in everyday leadership practice? I would like to illustrate this using a situation described by a manager: He works as a divisional manager in the food industry and reports on an experience that took place shortly after two divisions were merged. He had taken over the management of the newly created division shortly beforehand. During a regular staff meeting, he was suddenly confronted with the following situation:

> *"A visibly agitated employee comes into my office, closes the door, sits down, and starts talking. For around 20 minutes, he accuses me of everything that's going wrong, what wrong decisions I've made recently, and what could have been done better. The accusations are intense and personal."*

The divisional manager was completely surprised. The resistance hit him unprepared and with great force. The employee was unmistakably highly indignant, heaped accusations on the line manager, and initially gave him no room to take a stand. He let off steam and, because of the vehemence of the accusations, also saw the right on his side to present this to his superior. The resistance thus comes across as an open questioning of the person and therefore as a completely irreconcilable, personal rejection of the manager.

The divisional manager then tried to control his actions by suppressing the need to act out of emotion (getting angry, defensive, rejecting the other person, etc.) and first listening and giving the other person the opportunity to vent his anger. Then he tried to resume the conversation:

> *"I have to hold back a lot and manage to just listen and not get too emotionally charged. Afterwards, I try to take a stand on the various points, but I realize that completely different perspectives clash. I couldn't resolve it."*

The divisional manager fails in immediately resolving the obviously contradictory assessments. However, he acknowledges the differences that have come to light, does not directly reject them, and does not immediately condemn the position or viewpoint of the other person. His expression of opinion serves above all to make his point of view clear and to document the actual difference. By doing so, he fundamentally recognizes the employee's right to disagree and preserves the dignity of the other person by acknowledging their independence.

The conversation ended, but it kept the divisional manager very busy. On the one hand, he was still new in this role and the employee had been with the company for several years. Secondly, he was aware that this was his first time in a major management role and that he may well have made mistakes that he was not aware of. He allows for uncertainty by acknowledging the possibility that the employee's annoyance may be objectively justified and that the criticism of him may be at least partially correct. The resistance thus becomes, at least potentially, a justified difference of opinion and is not a priori devalued even if the manner of the accusation is hurtful and humiliating. In principle, the employee uses the discussion with the manager as an unannounced "pronouncement of judgment" and does not give the other person any opportunity to comment on the accusations in a differentiated manner or to come to a different judgment together.

The manager now set out to take a closer look at the situation and get a more comprehensive picture:

> *"Afterwards, I realized that the employee had also questioned my competence with other members of management and the managing director during my vacation absence."*

Further investigations revealed that the discussion with the employee was only the tip of the iceberg and was preceded by a comprehensive defamation of the divisional manager. The employee attempted to convince both the hierarchy and the employees of his negative assessment of the manager without the "condemned" person having been able to comment on it in advance. On closer inspection, it becomes clear that the employee's possibly justified criticism was staged as a power struggle against the divisional manager. The employee reversed the usual game. With his approach, he did not give his superior the opportunity to make his voice heard and worked against him behind his back by trying to forge a coalition against him and thus use others to support his convictions. This orchestrated power struggle served to get the superior out of the way and turn him into a victim of consummate intrigue. The employee ran the risk of damaging the superior's dignity as well as his own.

The divisional manager was aware that the factual criticism may have been justified, but the questioning of his person threatened to undermine his legitimacy as a manager. To be able to fulfill his management role at all, he had to find out whether he was still considered legitimate as a manager. He therefore actively clarified this by approaching the managing director who assured his support as well as from the management and the board of directors. He also learned from HR that the resistor had clear management aspirations and wanted his job. The result of the investigation showed that the hierarchy had legitimized him as a manager, and the assessment of the situation that the employee was attempting to undermine his legitimacy as a manager to gain an advantage for himself was reinforced.

The divisional manager then invited the employee to another discussion and prepared very well for it:

> *"I made my view of things clear and pointed out in no uncertain terms that I was the manager here and could only work with employees who accepted me as a manager and pulled in the same direction. I explained clearly that otherwise it would not be possible to work together, and that the employment relationship would have to be terminated."*

If you analyze this sequence, it becomes clear that the manager is only asking for one thing in this conversation: he expects the employee to recognize that he is the manager and holds this position. He does not reproach him, does not condemn his actions, and thus makes it possible for him to save face. However – and this is an important distinction – loyalty is not understood as obedience, but as acceptance of the person in the management position.

The divisional manager then described the outcome of the meeting as "very positive." The employee changed his behavior completely and has since accepted him as his superior:

> *"We are now a very well rehearsed team in the department and complement each other well. The employee in question is certainly still the most difficult person to manage but is fully committed to the company and generally does a good job. If we have differences today, it's often due to different ways of thinking and perspectives, but I can live with that."*

The superior does not respond. He does not list all the offenses, does not show him up, and therefore does not portray him as an intruder. In this way, there is no discussion about past events; the employee does not have to justify himself and can save face. The line manager respects and upholds the dignity of the other person. He only requires the employee to respect his position as a manager and to behave loyally in this respect, but he does not deny him his right to continue to express criticism. Despite this difficult starting position, it is thus possible for differences of opinion to be allowed and for constructive cooperation and learning to take place within the team.

## 7.3 Artfully Confronting Resistance

Let us now take a further final step in terms of dealing with resistance. When it comes to design recommendations, as in this section, very specific instructions for action are repeatedly proposed, which, according to the authors, must then be followed in a linear order. These lists may offer certainty, but they are also deceptive. The fact is . . .

> "*as if we were sent out on a swaying rope stretched over a precipice (. . .) and given no other advice than this: hold on tight!*"

In this regard, Robert Musil (1987, p. 770) formulated rigid, schematic moral guidelines that resemble concrete instructions for action in their basic pattern. They offer something very important: they tell us how to behave correctly in certain situations. But the price of certainty is that the person acting then applies a template and runs the risk of not engaging sufficiently with the situation. But that is exactly what is needed, because every situation is different, which has already become clear from the wide variety of resistance situations described in this book. In addition, people and the relationships between them differ greatly. Does a person apply a template correctly, does he or she not observe, think, and act for himself or herself, but tend to concentrate on correctly reproducing the supposedly appropriate template? Moreover, specific instructions for action are always based on assumptions, which are often justified by the long practical experience of the person proposing them. Experience is important and should be recognized, no question, but its substance need not be beyond doubt. The templates can be constructive, future-oriented, solution-oriented, but also destructive, punitive, nonsensical, cynical, or destructive. It is therefore crucial that the individual examines *their own* underlying, often self-evident basic assumptions, reflects on them, and develops them further. This is the breeding ground from which behavioral patterns grow in everyday life and from which managers can gain self-confidence.

Therefore, no conclusive, concrete instructions for action that are helpful in all situations are to be expected here. Rather, what follows are references to a "certain way of leading," which is linked to a certain "way of living" (Bieri 2013) (i.e. with a chosen, specific view of oneself and the world and relationships that surround oneself). When reflecting on the cases and the question of how certain resistance could have been avoided or how a productive dynamic could have emerged from situations of resistance, I gradually came up with specific pointers that I see as maxims for action. They build on the leadership principles and presuppose them. They are not social technologies; rather, you have to be intentional about them. If the sincere confrontation with resistance is only staged, it can be assumed that it will not be authentic and will be experienced as an act.

Resistance is not simply a factual problem that can be countered with sufficient reason and rational argumentation. Strong emotions play a role because people are angry or hold opposing views with verve. And then people are pitted against people, which means that the resisters often take a risk and those who are attacked feel threatened because they are called into question as individuals. If a manager wants to deal with resistance in the way described here, they will expect unpredictability. They will assume that not everything can be penetrated and understood and that there is no completely rational, plannable set of behaviors that will guide them through the imponderable situation. Instead, they will move through the resistance situation with an alert eye, a clear attitude, and an open mind.

## Attentiveness

As we have seen, one of the major pitfalls in dealing with resistance is jumping to conclusions. The attentiveness mindset counters this impulse. Organizational experts Weick and Sutcliffe (2010, p. 36) place a high value on mindfulness "because it counteracts the tendency to interpret events as something familiar and thus simplify them (the tendency to normalize) and strengthens the tendency to redefine and interpret events as something less familiar. Less mindful practices normalize; mindful practices anomalize – and by *anomalizing* we mean that mindfulness draws attention to characteristic peculiarities and thus slows down the pace at which details are declared normal."

But how can this be achieved? How can I move in unforeseen situations without committing myself quickly and conclusively and thus depriving myself and the others involved of important options for thought and action? We are probably all familiar with the appeasing and defensive response: "I appreciate you being so clear. I understand your arguments very well, but we also have to take this [and that] into account." This is a tactical response that suggests I have listened carefully without actually having done so. I'm tricking the other person, letting them go nowhere, as I'm not referring to them at all, but only pretending to take them seriously. Just wanting to give the other person the feeling that I am taking them seriously is not enough. Without the feeling that the other person is right or that something new can come to light that is relevant, and without this curiosity, the genuine, authentic interest in the other person (i.e. mindfulness) is inconceivable.

The advice to simply listen better or to switch on all my senses is not enough if I am unable to really engage with the situation and the other person. I have to be fully present in the situation – a demanding requirement when I'm stressed or barraged with criticism in the presence of others. But even when things are difficult, I listen to the other person or look at them without immediately judging what I hear or see and without letting my own feelings (anger, resentment, rage, insecurity) get the better of me. It is not intuition or a spontaneous feeling that leads me to withdraw because of a demand that seems excessive at first glance or to flare up because of the audacity of the rebellious other person. I look, listen, and follow the thoughts, arguments, and emotions of the other person.

In the previous chapter, the manager describes it as follows: "I have to hold back a lot and manage to just listen and not get too emotionally charged either." The listener leaves their own point of view, their usual place, at the moment of listening. It is also difficult because I am often addressed directly as a person. This usually triggers a reaction: justification. The process of listening mutates into an opportunity to organize a response. I collect the counterarguments to the accusations made and prepare a response strategy. By contrast, a mindful approach suggests sticking to what I am currently perceiving, not digressing, staying with the other person, their words and their expression and taking this in. Attention is needed at a moment when someone turns against me and my arguments.

## Exploring at Eye Level

One major concern that may arise from the demand for mindfulness is that I won't "come to myself" because of all the listening (i.e. I won't be able to collect myself and have my answer or reaction ready in time). In addition, management is traditionally expected to be able to grasp situations quickly and make decisions. It makes sense for managers to get an overview, sort things out, assess the situation, and thus reach a decision. However, the decisive factor is how quickly this is done. If this process is too quick, it is premature, rushed, and biased. The manager cannot be surprised, already knows everything, has lost curiosity. But this also means they are unable to penetrate the situation mentally. In situations of resistance, this form of certainty and authority is of little help; what is needed is the willingness to acknowledge the lack of knowledge, the lack of penetration of the situation and to rely on the fact that this knowledge and penetration are not simply and always there but must be increasingly and repeatedly re-established. Dealing with resistance is therefore largely also about recognizing and accepting uncertainty. In a conversation with a management consultant, he once told me that at the beginning he often had the feeling that he simply didn't know anything, that he had no idea where the journey was going. This feeling at the beginning of a consulting situation stayed with him over all the years of management consulting and he couldn't get rid of it. It's like artists' stage fright before a performance. In my opinion, this insecurity is not an expression of weakness that needs to be covered up, but rather a true strength to allow and accept this feeling and not try to "turn it off." Because without this feeling, no curious journey of exploration can take place.

What is the exploration about? As we have seen, especially with hasty conclusions, managers often see resistance as something that arises in others, is justified, and, above all, has nothing to do with them. The consequences of this are sufficiently described in this book. But what can be done now? In my opinion, a more precise exploration of the leadership relationships and the respective contribution of the various participants to the situation that is interpreted as a resistance situation is required. The word "interpret" is relevant because it "is" not resistance, but the situation is "interpreted" as such.

And how can such an exploration take place? Mindfulness involves leaving your own position and being able to put yourself in the other person's shoes. When it comes to exploring the relationship in more detail, it is also necessary to better understand who has made what contribution to the situation, and this is only possible if this happens at eye level (i.e. if I allow the other person to talk about my perceived contribution and this perception is significant in itself). This does not mean that I agree with the perception, but it does mean that I do not assume a priori that the perception is not correct anyway or that it cannot claim legitimacy.

And that is the real heroic act. Management does not mean being the rock in the sea, defying all adversity and standing firm.

But management also does not mean giving up the asymmetry in decision-making authority; rather, this must be accepted. The participants are then not on an equal footing, but they are of equal value. Without this differentiation in power relations, management and the organization lack an essential prerequisite for effectiveness. However, this asymmetry does not derive its legitimacy from insisting on one's own opinion, but from the ability to constantly re-establish this authority. Rudolf Wimmer (2009, p. 29 et seq.) formulates this as follows: "Today, it is a personal achievement of management to bring about a common will from situation to situation and to create the necessary basis of acceptance for this, despite all willingness to negate and dissent." In situations of resistance, this means not knowing everything from the outset, having all the reaction patterns ready and being able to make a decision immediately. Instead, management means initiating and carefully shaping a clarification and communication process. At the end of this process, the manager makes a decision that is considered sensible, is supported, and is also sustainable. The aim of this process is to ensure that different perspectives, interests, and concerns can be taken into account and negotiated, and that the management can make more prudent decisions if the original decision has been questioned. This does not mean that the previous decision is automatically put up for discussion, but it does mean that it can be modified.

Acting prudently as a manager means focusing on your own role and task and always realizing that you need to think in terms of processes. And that takes time. However, this does not mean simply taking your time with answers. Resistance arises in situations of high urgency and relevance. Just as resistors have a right to object, they do not have a right to have their request granted, but they do have a right to be informed that their request has been received and when they will be informed again about how to proceed in this matter. Anything else increases the resisters' sense of risk and can give the impression that their request is being put on the back burner.

## Turning People into Doers

There are two components to the communication process: firstly, exploring why a resistance situation could arise in the first place and secondly, finding new solutions. Achieving this exploration at eye level means involving those who resist (i.e. those who have clear demands), those who are against it at first glance, but also those who have taken themselves out of the process. When employees in organizations feel dependent and powerless, it is not simply the management which is at fault. The members of the organization who feel like victims also contribute to this themselves. The task of management is not to lament the victim mentality, but to create the framework conditions and do everything possible to ensure that the members of the organization can get involved and thus become "doers" (i.e. people who actively help shape the process).

Clarifying the dynamics of resistance is complex and can only be made accessible if those involved are open to the perspectives of others. This process of reflection involves a differentiated weighing up of all the different parts. In this weighing up, care must be taken not to automatically overweight one part. For example, it is important to avoid immediately taking responsibility in the hope of calming the situation or automatically looking for someone to blame and then always automatically blaming others. Instead, the situation should be carefully examined and explored through the following questions:

- What characterizes the current situation?
- How do the various participants experience the resistance?
- How do I view my and the other person's role in the resistance?

- How does the other person see their and my role in the resistance?

- How can I make it clear that I stand by my mistakes without every mistake automatically calling the decision into question?

- What options are there for shaping the process to create a productive dynamic?

As the many examples in this book have shown, a key result of such explorations is that the causes of an unsatisfactory situation are nuanced and do not clearly stem from one person. From a management perspective, it then makes sense not to attribute the fault to the other person and not to place the deficit there ("you didn't do a good job"), but to assume causality ("it is important to me [in my role as a manager], I want it this way and ask you to do it this way in the future") and to take and defend a position authentically.

When it comes to looking for new solutions, not only those who have resisted, but also those who have only expressed themselves in a covert way should be addressed directly and encouraged to get involved. Management should therefore create opportunities for participation and not simply impose change (Dent and Goldberg 1999, p. 36). It is all too easy to resign oneself to the statement that it was simply "not possible." However, this can quickly become a protective claim that insufficient thought was given to how such participation could have been organized. However, as mentioned above, the dignity of others is endangered or elementary principles of fairness are disregarded, which are not written down anywhere, but are part of the unspoken contract with the organization. Members of the organization expect the following, as a study of managers and employees (Kim and Mauborgne 2003 or Ford et al. 2008) shows:

- **Participation** means involving people in decisions that affect them. They should be invited to contribute and be allowed to refute each other's ideas and assumptions. In this way, management expresses respect for the individual.

- **Explanation** means that everyone involved or affected should understand why final decisions are made exactly as they are. An explanation and clarification of the reasoning gives people confidence that managers have at least considered their opinions and made the decision impartially and in the overall interests of the company.

- **Clarity of expectations** requires that managers explain the new framework conditions or rules after a decision has been made, even if these are challenging. Employees should know in advance the new requirements based on which they will be assessed.

Ideally, the qualified result or suitable variants emerge from within the organization. Those who participate (in whatever form) help define the new purpose and are also recognized as an end in themselves, as they are made part of the solution.

## Perseverance

There is a fine line between persistent, persevering, consistent, and predictable and stubborn, unrelenting, and categorical. It is certainly easier to insist on something when it has been consensually agreed than when it has been unilaterally imposed. I would like to understand persistence here as sticking to a conviction or decision if it proves to still be sensible, appropriate, or reasonable after sufficient exploration and participation. If the decision proves to be inappropriate, excessively restrictive, or even harmful, then it probably makes sense to revise it. But a decision should not be revised without necessity, as this can create the impression of a lack of stability and unpredictability. So does the manager change their mind for the sake of harmony because the current situation simply dictates it without justification, or because they feel closer to their employees and this closeness gives them the feeling that they are accepted by their employees and indeed a little bit loved? All these examples show that the person is guided at this moment by a vague good feeling of doing the right thing, without having the implication for the management role in mind. Something is implicitly traded: the gain is the feeling of well-being, the reduction of tension, the distance, and the impression of having gained closeness. The loss may be that the management then makes arbitrary, unfounded decisions and is therefore no longer predictable. The price of perseverance is the perceived distance, not being the same as others, not simply being appreciated or even loved, but the gain of perseverance is being tangible as a manager. This is because a persistent manager only puts a decision up for discussion against a background of good reasons and then justifies the revision of the decision in a comprehensible manner.

## 7.4  Artfully Evoking Resistance

Managers also exhibit resistance, as we have seen in various examples. Both the view of resistance and the recommendations for dealing with resistance are made from a managerial perspective. The perspective of the resistors is neglected (Courpasson et al. 2012, p. 803). So, what should middle managers take into account when putting up resistance, assuming that this resistance should be effective? In this section, I will only deal with the obvious resistance when managers suddenly want to express their demands to a management level higher up or to top management. In my opinion, this is where there is the greatest scope and need for action and the opportunity to channel resistance into productive channels.

I assume that middle management will put up resistance in the form of explicit demands when it comes to essential issues and values in the organization. The aim is not to question or weaken top management, but rather for middle management to temporarily interact with top management on an equal footing. Middle management is also not simply concerned with resisting change, but with initiating change or giving change a different direction.

It cannot be assumed that top management deals productively with resistance from middle management because it is itself particularly competent or benevolent, but because of the competence of the resisters. They must resist skillfully and prudently. This includes the following two points (Courpasson et al. 2012, p. 802, 816 et seq.), but certainly also persistence. Resistors can give up too quickly, as we saw in the case of the two managers from the transportation industry, behind whose backs two employees were poached for another department (see section 2.1). They allow themselves to be led too much by moral indignation or strong disappointments and so their resistance fizzles out ineffectively.

## Organizing Legitimation

One problem that is often encountered when dealing with resistance is the attribution of resistance to certain individuals, groups, or organizational units. If the same people resist again and again, top management expects resistance, knows it's coming, classifies it, and devalues it. It's always the same people anyway, they are against it on principle, they only show solidarity with the losers or do so out of a sense of duty. This means that resisters lose legitimacy before a cause has even been voiced. This also means that this symbolic component must be of particular importance. In the example of the bank (see section 2.1), the resistance group is formed from particularly high-performing branch managers for precisely this reason. In other words, those who offer resistance should ask themselves who or which group must stand up for it to lend legitimacy to the cause.

It is therefore helpful if managers have strong, resilient relationships at the same management level and across management levels to be prepared in the event that they themselves put up resistance. If it is then possible to organize a support group, it is also possible to address top management directly and lodge a protest there.

## Speaking the Language of Management

Whose language should the resisters speak? It is clear from various studies that management only really pays attention to resisters when they understand how to adopt the perspective of the management or speak the language of the management. In relation to top management, middle management has advantages because they are closer to top management than employees without a management function and therefore have more insight into their world. Resistors should try to put themselves in management's shoes and formulate their complaint in such a way that the situation, which they see as unsatisfactory, also appears unsatisfactory and problematic from the management's perspective. In other words, the content of the complaint must be compatible with the management's point of view and the management must be able to accept it.

The complaint must have a rational basis and the usual practices must be observed: analysis of the situation, justification of specific complaints, and a list of concrete suggestions as to how the situation can be improved. It is important to consider whether it is better to make concrete demands or to call for a genuine willingness to talk and negotiate. It should be borne in mind that those to whom a complaint is addressed appreciate it just as little as the resistors themselves when their freedom is taken away from them.

But what about emotions? Can or should emotions be involved? As already shown in the examples in section 6.2, issues and emotions are inseparable. If someone presents a matter with enthusiasm, this is usually evaluated positively. Emotions that are specifically observed or attributed are evaluated negatively: for example, if a superior feels unjustly attacked or embarrassed, if a superior gains the impression that others have nothing but contempt for them and mock them, or if the manager has the impression that the resistors are wallowing in self-pity and withdrawing in resignation. Then the attacked person easily loses respect for the attackers. It is probably not a question of resistors presenting their complaint with purely factual arguments and without emotion. They are resisting because they fundamentally disagree with something (for example, a decision or behavior of the management). And that is upsetting. For resistors, this means firstly that the concern should also be understandable for those to whom the complaint is addressed, and secondly that the concern is presented convincingly, emphatically, and with commitment. Only with emotionality does it become clear that the complaint is of great importance to the resisters, and only then does the complaint become a genuine, authentic concern that the resisters expect to be taken seriously. Nevertheless, emotionality remains an Achilles' heel of resistance to this day, as emotions are often not seen as an important form of expression but are often misused as a reproach to deprive a complaint of its legitimacy.

For the management to accept a complaint, the discussion situation should be designed appropriately. In principle, a balance should be struck between informal, exploratory discussions and formal, written complaints, such as those made to the bank (see section 2.1). In informal discussions, the complaint does not immediately become public, and the manager is more likely to see themselves as part of the problem-solving process. However, there is also a risk that concerns will not be given sufficient weight and will fizzle out again. At the bank, the complaint had a formal character, was made public within the organization, and was addressed directly to top management, bypassing the directly superior management level. In this way, the concern was emphasized, but the risk of an open power struggle was also taken. It is often not a question of whether one or the other approach is chosen. In some situations, it is also appropriate to proceed both informally and formally.

## 7.5 Artfulness and Resistance: A Final Reflection

I have repeatedly used the term "art" or "artfulness" in the headings but have not yet justified it. I don't want to get into a debate here about what is meant by art. Others can make more qualified comments on this. I understand "art" or "artfulness" in this chapter simply as a metaphor that helps to understand and formulate the management's approach to resistance in a certain way.

As can be seen in this book, resistance is not a clear and well-defined phenomenon. Resistance is nuanced. It is used tactically as a term and can be traced back to a complex relationship dynamic. It is the same with artistic objects or forms of representation. They live from being interpreted, and the meaning of art shifts or changes depending on the viewer, the context, and the time of viewing. Their charm lies in the fact that they are not closed, but open and alive. My plea to management is to meet resistance with an open mind, not to try to grasp and explain the situation quickly and conclusively with hasty conclusions, and not to fall prey to promisingly advertised "practical guides." Rather, the management should engage with the situation described as resistance, get involved in the situation, and remain curious to better understand what is going on. It is therefore not about applying a "correct" yardstick for the "right" way to deal with resistance, but about constantly finding, or rather inventing, one's own measure and appropriate responses. It's about what significance the resistance situation has for you and the others involved. Art is also about creative design in the confrontation with oneself and what surrounds the artist. *Designing together with* the people involved in resistance situations must be clearly distinguished from the *application of* prefabricated social technologies *to* the resisters.

When it comes to recipes, I like to cook those that say "Always works." Unfortunately, there is no recipe for dealing with resistance, and dealing with resistance does not always "work." Nevertheless, dealing with resistance – as in cooking, as in art – requires skills and abilities or those that develop over time, but are never finished or completed. I rarely meet managers who say they now know "how to lead." Management and leadership are a constant learning process, which certainly also involves specific technical skills. But for the most part – as in art – it is about constantly exploring and adopting new perspectives and not letting go of this search.

Resistance is sometimes exhausting, as is art. But both invigorate and make life richer.

## Summary

- When considering resistance, four leadership principles are proposed, all of which must be taken into account if resistance is to be handled carefully and productively: leadership relationships or relationships in general should be lived with commitment, the dignity of the other person should be respected and preserved, the other person should be granted the right to dissent, and people as well as organizations should be viewed and treated in such a way that learning and development is possible.

- Managing resistance situations means meeting them prudently with mindfulness, allowing an authentic and honest exchange to take place at eye level, dealing with people in organizations in such a way that they experience themselves as doers and not as victims, and that management is experienced as persistent but not stubborn.

- When it comes to putting up effective resistance yourself, there are two main issues: firstly, you should try to legitimize your concerns based on the personal constellation of support. Secondly, it is important to understand the logic and requirements of the management as well as possible to be able to speak "their" language.

- "Art" or "artful" can be used as a metaphor to illustrate a process and development-oriented approach to resistance.

# Sources

## Literature

Ashforth, B.E. and Mael, F.A. (1998). The power of resistance. Sustaining valued identities. In: *Power and Influence in Organizations* (ed. R.M. Kramer and M.A. Neale), 89–119. Thousand Oaks: Sage.

Athanassov, Y. (2014). Im Lichte der Doppelrolle. Neue Zürcher Zeitung. Weiterbildung und Karriere. Auf Bildungsreise. Ansichten zur höheren Weiterbildung. Sonderbeilage (5 November).

Baitsch, C. (1993). *Was bewegt Organisationen? Selbstorganisation aus psychologischer Perspektive*. Frankfurt a. M.: Campus.

Baitsch, C. and Nagel, E. (2014). Organisationskultur – das verborgene Skript der Organisation. In: *Praktische Organisationswissenschaft. Lehrbuch für Studium und Beruf*, 2nd ed. (ed. J.O. Meissner, R. Wimmer, and P. Wolf), 267–288. Heidelberg: Carl-Auer-Verlag.

Baumgartner, F. (2014). Whistleblower-Prozess unterbrochen. Rudolf Elmer erleidet Zusammenbruch. Neue Zürcher Zeitung (12 October).

Baumgartner, F. (2015). Whistleblower-Prozess in Zürich. Bezirksgericht spricht Rudolf Elmer teilweise frei (19 January). http://www.nzz.ch/zuerich/bezirksgericht-spricht-rudolf-elmer-teilweise-frei-1.18464036.

Beer, M., Eisenstat, R., and Spector, B. (1990). Why change programs don't produce change. *Harvard Business Review* 67 (6): 58–166.

Behrens, M. (2013). Employment regulation in national contexts – Germany. In: *Comparative Employment Relations in the Global Economy* (ed. C. Frege and J. Kelly), 206–226. London/New York: Routledge.

Bieri, P. (2013). *Eine Art zu leben. Über die Vielfalt menschlicher Würde*. München: Carl Hanser.

Bömelburg, H.-J. (2011). Der andere Untertan. "Die Abenteuer des braven Soldaten Schwejk" von Jaroslav Hašek (1921–1923). In: *Literatur, die Geschichte schrieb* (ed. D. von Laak), 182–197. Göttingen: Vandenhoeck and Ruprecht.

Bovey, W.H. and Hede, A. (2000). Resistance to organizational change: The role of defence mechanisms. *Journal of Managerial Psychology* 16 (7): 534–548.

Brehm, J.W. (1966). *A Theory of Psychological Reactance*. New York: Academic Press.

Brehm, S.S. and Brehm, J.W. (1981). *Psychological Reactance: A Theory of Freedom and Control*. New York: Academic Press.

Coch, L. and French, J.R.P. (1948). Overcoming resistance to change. *Human Relations* 1: 512–532.

Cohn, A., Fehr, E., and Maréchal, M.A. (2014). Business culture and dishonesty in the banking industry. *Nature* 516: S. 86–89.

Contu, A. (2008). Decaf resistance. On misbehavior, cynicism, and desire in liberal workplaces. *Management Communication Quarterly* 21 (3): 364–397.

Courpasson, D. and Clegg, S. (2012). The Polyarchic bureaucracy: Cooperative resistance in the workplace and the construction of a new political structure of organizations. *Research in the Sociology of Organizations* 34: 55–79.

Courpasson, D., Dany, F., and Clegg, S. (2012). Resisters at work: Generating productive resistance in the workplace. *Organization Science* 23 (3): 801–819.

Crozier, M. and Friedberg, E. (1993). *Die Zwänge kollektiven Handelns. Über Macht und Organisation*. Frankfurt a. Main/Hain: Neue Wissenschaftliche Bibliothek.

Cunha, M.P.E., Clegg, S.R., Rego, A. et al. (2013). From the physics of change to realpolitik: Improvisational relations of power and resistance. *Journal of Change Management* 13 (4): 460–476.

Dent, E.B. and Goldberg, S.G. (1999). Challenging "resistance to change." *Journal of Applied Behavioral Science* 35 (1): 25–41.

De Wit, B. and Meyer, R. (2004). *Strategy. Process, Content, and Context*. London: Thomson Learning.

Edwards, P., Collinson, D., and Della Rocca, D. (1995). Workplace resistance in Western Europe: A preliminary overview and a research agenda. *European Journal of Industrial Relations* 1 (3): 283–316.

Eisenhardt, K.M., Furr, N.R., and Bingham, C. (2010). Microfoundations of performance: Balancing efficiency and flexibility in dynamic environments. *Organization Science* 21 (6): 1263–1273.

Endrissat, N. and Müller, W.R. (2007). Führung in Spitälern – Führungsverständnisse von Managern und Medizinern im Vergleich. WWZ Summary (June).

Endrissat, N., Müller, W.R., and Avery, G. (2007): Leadership according to professionals. An explorative study among chief physicians in Switzerland. Proceedings of the Australian and New Zealand Academy of Management Conference.

Evrard, J.S. (2014). Seita: les salariés de Carquefou arrêtent leur grève de la faim. *Le Parisien* (15 October).

Fineman, S. (2006). Emotion and organizing. In: *The Sage Handbook of Organization Studies* (ed. S.R. Clegg, C. Hardy, T.B. Lawrence et al.), 675–700. London/Thousand Oaks/New Delhi: Sage.

Fiol, C.M. and O'Conner, E.J. (2002). When hot and cold collide in radical change processes: Lessons from community development. *Organization Science* 13 (5): 532–546.

Fleming, P. (2007). Sexuality, power and resistance. *Organization Studies* 28 (2): 239–256.

Fleming, P. and Sewell, G. (2002). Looking for the good soldier, Švejk: Alternative modalities of resistance in the contemporary workplace. *Sociology* 36 (4): 857–873.

Fleming, P. and Spicer, A. (2003). Working at a cynical distance: Implications for power, subjectivity and resistance. *Organization* 10 (1): 157–179.

Fleming, P. and Spicer, A. (2008). Beyond power and resistance: New approaches to organizational politics. *Management Communication Quarterly* 21 (3): 301–309.

Ford, J.D., Ford, L.W., and D'Amelio, A. (2008). Resistance to change: The rest of the story. *Academy of Management Review* 2 (33): 362–377.

Gergen, K. (1999). *An Invitation to Social Construction*. London: Sage.

Gigerenzer, G. (2008). *Bauchentscheidungen. Die Intelligenz des Unbewussten und die Macht der Intuition*. München: Goldmann.

Gigerenzer, G. and Gaissmaier, W. (2006). Denken und Urteilen unter Unsicherheit: Kognitive Heuristiken. In: *Enzyklopädie der Psychologie. Kognition. 8. Denken und Problemlösen* (ed. J.F. Funke), 329–374. Göttingen/Bern/Toronto/Seattle: Hogrefe.

Glasl, F. (2013). *Konfliktmanagement. Ein Handbuch für Führungskräfte, Beraterinnen und Berater*, 11th ed. Stuttgart: Haupt.

Goffman, E. (1961). *Encounters*. Indianapolis: Bobbs-Merrill.

Grint, K. (2010). *Leadership. A Very Short Introduction*. New York: Oxford University Press.

Grugulis, I. (2002). Nothing serious? Candidates' use of humor in management training. *Human Relations* 55 (4): 387–406.

Hašek, J. (2013). *Die Abenteuer des braven Soldanten Schwejk 1 und 2*, 40th ed. Hamburg: Rowohlt.

Häubi, R. and Weber, W. (2004). Kollektive Arbeitsstreitigkeiten des Jahres 2003. *Schweizer Volkswirtschaft – Das Magazin für Wirtschaftspolitik* 11: 47–49.

Heintze, D. (2010). Smart und markig. Die Zeit (9 September) 37. https://www.zeit.de/2010/37/P-Brouwer.

Jermier, J.M. (1988). Sabotage at work: The rational view. *Research in the Sociology of Organizations* 6: 101–134.

Jermier, J.M. (1998). Introduction: Critical perspective on organizational control. *Administrative Science Quarterly* 43 (2): 235–256.

Jermier, J.M., Knights, D., and Nord, W.R. (1994). Resistance and power in organizations: Agency, subjectivity and the labour process. In: *Resistance and Power in Organizations* (ed. J.M. Jermier, D. Knights, and W.R. Nord), 2–24. New York: Routledge.

Kahneman, D. (2011). *Schnelles Denken, langsames Denken*. München: Siedler.

Kärreman, D. and Alvesson, M. (2009). Resisting resistance: Counter-resistance, consent and compliance in a consulting firm. *Human Relations* 62 (8): 1115–1144.

Kerber, K. and Buono, A.F. (2005). Rethinking organizational change: Reframing the challenge of change management. *Organization Development Journal* 23 (3): 23–38.

Kim, W.C. and Mauborgne, R. (2003). Fair process: Managing in the knowledge economy. *Harvard Business Review* 81 (January): 127–136.

Knowles, E.S. and Linn, J.A. (2004a). The importance of resistance to persuasion. In: *Resistance and Persuasion* (ed. E.S. Knowles and J.A. Linn), 3–9. Mahwah, NJ: Lawrence Erlbaum Associates.

Knowles, E.S. and Linn, J.A. (2004b). The promise and future of resistance and persuasion. In: *Resistance and Persuasion* (ed. E.S. Knowles and J.A. Linn), 301–310. Mahwah, NJ: Lawrence Erlbaum Associates.

Krantz, J. (1999). Comment on "Challenging 'resistance to change.'" *Journal of Applied Behavioral Science* 35 (1): 42–44.

Kunda, G. (1992). *Engineering Culture: Control and Commitment in a High-tech Corporation*. Philadelphia: Temple University Press.

Langer, M.-A. (2014). Geheimes Wettrüsten im Cyberspace. *Neue Zürcher Zeitung* 13/14 (December 2014) 290. http://www.nzz.ch/meinung/kommentare/geheimes-wettruesten-im-cyberspace-1.18443493 (accessed 6 April 2015).

LaNuez, D. and Jermier, J.M. (1994). Sabotage by managers and technocrats. In: *Resistance and Power in Organizations* (ed. J.M. Jermier, D. Knights, and W.R. Nord), 219–251. London: Routledge.

Lawrence, P.R. (1954). How to deal with resistance to change. *Harvard Business Review* 32 (3): 49–57.

Lesch, H. (2009). Erfassung und Entwicklung von Streiks in OECD-Ländern. IW-Trends (January). Köln: Institut der deutschen Wirtschaft.

Lovallo, D. and Kahneman, D. (2003). Delusions of success: How optimism undermines executives' decisions. *Harvard Business Review* 81 (July): 56–63. https://hbr.org/2003/07/delusions-of-success-how-optimism-undermines-executives-decisions.

Löhr, J. (2010). Mittleres Management. Die Leiden der Sandwich-Chefs. *Frankfurter Allgemeine*. Beruf and Chance (4 May). http://www.faz.net/aktuell/beruf-chance/arbeitswelt/mittleres-management-die-leiden-der-sandwich-chefs-1964960.html (accessed 19 December 2014).

Machfus, N. (1996). *Zwischen den Palästen*. Zürich: Unionsverlag. (Aus dem Arabischen von Doris Kilias, Originalausgabe 1956).

Müller, W.R. and Endrissat, N. (2006). Was bedeutet Führung in der Schweiz? WWZ News 30 (June).

Müller, W.R. and Hurter, M. (1999). Führung als Schlüssel zur organisationalen Lernfähigkeit. In: *Managementforschung 9: Führung – neu gesehen* (ed. G. Schreyögg and J. Sydow), 1–54. Berlin/New York: Walter de Gruyter.

Müller, W.R. and Widmer, W. (1989). Beziehungsorientierte Arbeitsgestaltung. In: *Die Aufgabe der Personalabteilung in einer sich wandelnden Umwelt* (ed. C. Lattmann and J. Krulis-Randa), S. 69–93. Heidelberg: Physica-Verlag.

Musil, R. (1987). *Der Mann ohne Eigenschaften*, vol. 1. Reinbek: Rowoholt.

Nagel, E. (2001). *Verwaltung anders denken*. Nomos: Baden-Baden.

Nagel, E. and Holzer, J. (2012). Praxis und Theorie – das eine geht nicht ohne das andere. (Theory and Practice – You Can't Have One Without the Other.) IBR-Arbeitsbericht (June/July). Luzern: Hochschule Luzern – Wirtschaft, Institut für Betriebs- und Regionalökonomie IBR.

Neuberger, O. (1995). *Mikropolitik – Der alltägliche Aufbau und Einsatz von Macht in Organisationen*. Stuttgart: Ferdinand Enke.

Ortmann, G. (2011). Moralverdrängung in und durch Organisationen. *Positionen* (Heft 3): 1–8.

Piderit, S.K. (2000). Rethinking resistance and recognizing ambivalence: A multidimensional view of attitudes towards organizational change. *Academy of Management Review* 25 (4): 783–794.

Prasad, P. and Prasad, A. (2000). Stretching the iron cage: The constitution and implications of routine workplace resistance. *Organization Science* 11(4): 387–403.

Prosinger, J. (2013). Zwischen Helden- und Verrätertum: Das Dilemma des Whistleblowers. *Der Tagesspiegel* 25 (August).

Raab, G., Unger, A., and Unger F. (2010). *Die Theorie psychologischer Reaktanz*. Wiesbaden: Gabler.

Radcliffe-Brown, A. (1952). *Structure and Function in Primitive Society*. London: Dohen and West.

Robins, S.R. and Judge, T.A. (2013). *Organizational Behavior*, 15th ed. (Boston: Pearson).

Rosenfelder, A. (2003). Arbeitskampf. Alle Mägen stehen still. *Frankfurter Allgemeine* (13 May). http://www.faz.net/aktuell/feuilleton/arbeitskampf-alle-maegen-stehen-still-1103519.html (accessed 21 November 2014).

Rothschild, J. and Miethe, T.D. (1994). Whistleblowing as resistance in modern work organizations; the politics of revealing organizational deception and abuse. In: *Resistance and Power in Organizations* (ed. J.M. Jermier, D. Knights, and W.R. Nord), 252–273. London: Routledge.

Schutz, A. (2004). Rethinking domination and resistance: Challenging post-modernism. *Educational Researcher* 33 (1): 15–23.

Scott, J. (1985). *Weapons of the Weak: Everyday Forms of Peasant Resistance*. New Haven, CT: Yale University Press.

Scott, J. (1986). Everyday forms of peasant resistance. *The Journal of Peasant Studies* 13 (2): 5–35.

Senge, P. (1990). *Fifth Discipline: The Art and Practice of the Learning Organization*. New York: Doubleday.

Shuler, S. and Sypher, B.D. (2000). Seeking emotional labor when managing the heart enhances the work experience. *Management Communication Quarterly* 14 (1): 50–89.

Spreitzer, G. M. and Quinn, R.E. (1996). Empowering middle managers to be transformational leaders. *Journal of Applied Behavioral Science* 32 (3): 237–261. https://doi.org/10.1177/0021886396323001.

Staehle, W.H. (1991). *Management. Eine verhaltenswissenschaftliche Perspektive*. München: Vahlen.

Sturdy, A. and Fineman, S. (2001). Struggles for the control of affect – resistance as politics and emotion. In: *Customer Service: Empowerment and Entrapment* (ed. A. Sturdy, I. Grugulis, and S.H. Willmott). 135–156. Basingstoke: Palgrave.

Symon. G (2005). Exploring resistance form a rhetorical perspective. *Organization Studies* 26 (11): 1641–1663.

Taylor, L. and Walton, P. (1971). Industrial sabotage: Motives and meanings. In: (Hrsg.). *Images of Deviance* (ed. S. Cohen), 219–245. Harmondsworth: Penguin.

Thompson, W.E. (1983). Hanging tongues: A sociological encounter with the assembly line. *Qualitative Sociology* 6 (3): 215–237.

Tornau, J.F. (2012). Arbeitskampf. Ausweitung der Kampfzone. *Magazin Mitbestimmung* (June).

Tucker, J. (1993). Everyday forms of employee resistance. *Sociological Forum* 8 (1): 25–45.

Vandaele, K. (2014). Ende des Abwärtstrends? Zur Entwicklung des Streikvolumens in Westeuropa seit Beginn der Weltwirtschaftskrise. *WSI Mitteilungen* (May): 345–352.

Vorauer, J.D., Cameron, J.C., Holmes, J.G. et al. (2003). Invisible overtures: Fear of rejection and the signal amplification bias. *Journal of Personality and Social Psychology* 84: 793–812.

Wagner, P. (2011). Am Ende nur noch zynisch. *Die Zeit* 17 (20 April).

Watzlawick, P., Beavin, J.H., and Jackson, D.D. (2011). *Menschliche Kommunikation: Formen, Störungen, Paradoxien*, 12th ed. Bern/Stuttgart/Wien: Huber.

Weick, K.E. (2000). Emergent change as a universal in organizations. In: *Breaking the Code of Change* (ed. M. Beer and N. Nohria), 223–241. Harvard Business Press.

Weick, K.E. and Sutcliffe, K.M. (2010). *Das Unerwartete managen: wie Unternehmen aus Extremsituationen lernen*, rev. ed. Stuttgart: Schäffer-Poeschel.

Westwood, R.I. (2004). Comic relief: Subversion and catharsis in organizational comedic theatre. *Organization Studies* 25 (5): 775–795.

Westwood, R. and Johnston, A. (2012). Reclaiming authentic selves: Control, resistive humor and identity work in the office. *Organization* 19 (6): 787–808.

Wimmer, R. (2009). Führung und Organisation – zwei Seiten ein und derselben Medaille. *Revue für postheroisches Management* (heft 4): 20–33.

# Web Links

to Chapter 3: TV series Die Abenteuer des braven Soldaten Schwejk (Folge 1): https://www.youtube.com/watch?v=OfMdakd4bHI (accessed 5 December 2014).

to section 3.1: Feature film Das Leben der Anderen: http://www.youtube.com/watch?v=CXQp9leFZFY (accessed 5 December 2014).

to section 3.3: Zeit auf dem Klo vertrödeln: www.spiegel.de/karriere/berufsleben/aufs-klo-gehen-bei-der-arbeit-us-firma-ueberwacht-zeit-auf-toilette-a-981637.html in: Karriere Spiegel from 17.07.2014 19:17 (accessed 3 December 2014).

to section 3.3: Einfallsreiches Trödeln: www.spiegel.de/forum/karriere/dienst-nach-vorschrift-lernen-vom-kollegen-faultier-thread-96777-1.html (accessed 3 December 2014).

to section 3.4: Rivalität zwischen Lionel Messi und Cristiano Ronaldo: www.goal.com/de/news/839/primera-division/2014/08/28/5066473/cristiano-ronaldo-rivalit%C3%A4t-mit-lionel-messi-ist-teil-meines (accessed 5 December 2014).

to section 3.6: Freistoßspray im Fußball: www.tagesschau.de/sport/freistoss-spray-bundesliga-101.html (accessed 8 December 2014); www.zeit.de/sport/2014-10/freistossspray-erfinder-heine-allemagne (accessed 8 December 2014).

to section 5.1: Video-Lerneinheit John Kotter: www.youtube.com/watch?v=Wdroj6F3VlQ (accessed 30 November 2014).

to section 5.5: US-Regierung gegen BP: www.tagesanzeiger.ch/panorama/vermischtes/Gewinn-und-Produktion-ueber-Sicherheit/story/21529289 (accessed 28 October 2014).

to section 6.2: Bahnarbeiter Phineas Gage: www.nzz.ch/aktuell/startseite/das-bildnis-des-phineas-gage-1.3522069 (accessed 17 December 2014).

# Acknowledgments

Many managers have told me their experiences on the subject of resistance. I have included some of these episodes in the book in an anonymous form. I would like to thank all these managers for taking the time. It was only thanks to their contributions that this book could be produced in its present form.

On the one hand, the book aims to understand resistance as an everyday phenomenon. However, the aim was not to simply reproduce the stories of managers, but to better understand typical experiences of resistance and to take a reflective look at them. Werner Müller supported me in interpreting the episodes described by managers. I would like to thank him for his precise and appreciative examination of the managers' stories and his stimulating thoughts on the subject. On the other hand, the book also aims to incorporate the scientific findings on resistance. Claudia Binz Astrachan supported me in the first phase of the research. At the EGOS conference in July 2014, Nada Endrissat provided me with further crucial information on academic contributions on the topic. Thanks to her support, I came across valuable research findings and relevant publications.

Once the text was in its first version, it had to pass the reading test. Dorin Kaiser and Urs Joss read the text very carefully and – in addition to positive feedback – did not spare me with critical and helpful comments, which led to some adjustments and revisions. Judith Henzmann from the Versus publishing house and Eva Bucher from the Institute for Business and Regional Economics (IBR) put the finishing touches to the text with their linguistic sensitivity. Many other people were interested in the topic, listened to me, shared their own experiences on the subject, and contributed one or two inspiring ideas: Franziska Baetcke, Regula Diehl, Michael Edele, Hannes Egli, Eric Facon, Timo Keller, Andreas Marfurt, Stefan Michel, Rehab Rashad, Vinzenz Rast, Beni Stocker, Leila Straumann, Katharina Windler.

The book is the result of my sabbatical from July 2014 to January 2015. I would like to thank the Kutlar-Joss family. They provided me with a room on the second floor of their house, known within the family as the hermitage. I was able to think and write there undisturbed. I also enjoyed the time with them and the conversations over a coffee artfully prepared by Urs Joss – conversations that are otherwise not possible in regular everyday life. I am grateful to my wife Dorin that we were able to enjoy our time together during the sabbatical and make this special everyday life so uncomplicated and respectful. My by then 10-year-old son, Maxim, seemed to be inspired by the idea that his father wanted to write a book; he also wrote one or two small books during this time. My 7-year-old daughter, Yma, started to get excited about letters during this time; she started reading her first book. It will probably be a while before she reads my book. However, she is already a proven expert in practicing resistance.

—Erik Nagel

# About the Author

Erik Nagel is interested in culturally sensitive management, leadership, and working relationships that develop between people in organizations and why people behave in this way and not differently. He looks behind the scenes of the organization with the aim of developing a constructive and learning-oriented culture. Erik Nagel's areas of expertise in teaching, consulting, and research are management, leadership, organizational culture, and change management. He is a lecturer at the Lucerne School of Business, program director for the Executive MBA Lucerne, and co-head of the Institute for Business and Regional Economics (IBR). He is also Vice Director of the Lucerne School of Business at Lucerne University of Applied Sciences and Art. Erik Nagel lives with his family in Basel.

# Index